Centre for
Liberty Report
on CANZUK

Taking CANZUK into the 2020s

Ciarán Reed

First published in Great Britain in 2021.

Copyright © 2021 by Ciarán Reed

All rights reserved. No part of this book may be reproduced in any form without the written permission of the author (Ciarán Reed)

ISBN   9798723028227.

Centre for Liberty Report on CANZUK

Table of Contents

Introduction 4

Anglosphere 13

Trade 31

Free Movement 41

Rights 51

International Problems 77

Foreign Policy by Consent 88

CANZUK at the United Nations 123

Joint Nuclear Deterrent 151

Conclusions 164

Bibliography 179

Ciarán Reed

Introduction

The intention of this policy paper is to move the debate around CANZUK in a new direction and suggest proposals beyond the already promoted and debated issues of tariff free trade and free movement.

CANZUK is a proposed union of the four kingdoms of Canada, Australia, New Zealand and the United Kingdom. The exact nature of the union is somewhat disputed, with most views generally including at least free trade but some stretching as far as furthering joint military operations. This paper will intend on giving a direction to that and set out a series of proposals and policies, which if implemented, would constitute an increase in cooperation and ties between the four CANZUK Kingdoms.

The history of the idea is somewhat disputed. Duncan Bell and Srdjan Vucetic have provided the best summary of the history of CANZUK, having written that it 'is at once new and old.' (Bell and Srdjan, 2019) In their article for the *British journal of politics & international relations* they simultaneously traced the idea of deeper ties between the four kingdoms through: the beliefs of the Imperial Federalist League, founded in 1884; the term to the 1960s; and the modern growth of the idea to Margaret Thatcher's appearances at the 1999 Conservative Party Conference (Bell and Srdjan, 2019). In doing so, Bell and Srdjan demonstrated how CANZUK can be both a 'new and old' (Bell and Srdjan, 2019) idea, with CANZUK representing a new iteration of the over 150-year-old idea that there should be some form of deeper union between Canada, Australia, New Zealand and the United Kingdom.

The recent debate around CANZUK has generally been seen in the context of the wider British question of European Union membership, with CANZUK supporters tending to come from the position of being Brexit backing individuals, such as Vote Leave Founder Daniel Hannan (now Lord Hannan [all individuals will be referred to by what title was held at time of the publication being referred to]) in the UK (Hannan, 2018, A) along with Brexiteer members of parliament such as Andrew Rosindell (Rosindell, 2021) and Michael Fabricant (Fabricant, 2017). That Brexit link is also true across the three new kingdoms that comprise of the proposed CANZUK union, with: David Seymour, the New Zealand

Act Party leader, writing his most accessible article on the issue for Brexit Central (Seymour, 2019); leading CANZUK advocate in the Australian Senate James Paterson (Paterson, 2020) having previously supported Brexit (Paterson, 2016); and in Canada from the then future (now former) Conservative Party of Canada leader Andrew Scheer (CANZUK International, 2017), a previous Brexit backer (Scheer, 2016).

It is not just supporters of CANZUK who come from only one side of the United Kingdom's European Union referendum. The anti-CANZUK caucus have also engaged on the topic through the prism of British membership of the European Union. Peter Geoghegan, an anti-Brexit political commentator, denounced 'Brexiters' (Geoghegan, 2020) for the supporting the idea of CANZUK, whilst Kevin Rudd's, the former Australian Prime Minister, article in the same newspaper about CANZUK was directed as well against 'the Brexiteers' (Rudd, 2019) and concluded that people should 'support legislation for a second referendum' (Rudd, 2019). This focus upon Brexit has dragged the debate around CANZUK into being a continuation of the 2016 British referendum.

Even outside of the four kingdoms, discussion on the topic of CANZUK is framed by Brexit, with Deutsche Welle releasing a report titled *'CANZUK — Could it be Britain's new EU?'* (Deutsche Welle, 2020). The intention of this policy paper is to take CANZUK out of the context of the Brexit debate and provide a framework to create a discourse beyond the politics of the 2010s. The debate on that topic is over with the British both formally and in practice outside of the European Union. Keeping the discussion on CANZUK based within the Brexit divide will: alienate large numbers of potential supporters of the idea who opposed or were not interested in Brexit; make the concept less relevant to the politics of the 2020s, potentially leading to it falling out of discussion; and limit the ideas entering into the concept through focusing on what the European Union does rather than on what CANZUK could do.

That shift away from the a British and Brexit focus to CANZUK will be done in three major ways. The first is simply through the timing of this report. The United Kingdom formally left the European Union and a new trade deal has been initiated between the European Union and the United Kingdom. This means that CANZUK is no longer an alternative to the European Union for the United Kingdom being argued for by those wishing to present it as an option for a post-leave world that they want or an object of attack to encourage people to support remaining in the European Union. As a result, such framing is no longer a part of the wider political landscape. That will allow this policy paper to avoid becoming tied to the debates and political movements of the 2016 referendum, as previous articles have when created during the aftermath of the British referendum.

Secondly, this paper will not attempt to compare CANZUK with the European Union. Advocates of the CANZUK model have a habit of explaining how it is different to the European Union. These include Hannan's speech to the Conservative Party of Canada Conference in 2018, where he compared the regulatory alignment procedures of the European Union with what he wanted from CANZUK, a regulation recognition trade agreement (Hannan, 2018, B); and Andrew Robertson's comparison that 'Unlike the EU, however, whose leaders refused to disclose its ultimate centralizing goals when it was set up in the 1950s, CANZUK would not seek an "ever closer union."' (Robertson, 2020) These comparisons to the European Union do not help explain CANZUK as it turns the CANZUK debate into an either-or choice about British Membership of the European Union, rather than an idea in its own right, making the debate on the topic devolve back to the Brexit issue, thereby discouraging support from people who had been against Brexit and making it less relevant to those in the three new kingdoms. This policy paper will intend to move beyond that by avoiding comparison with the European Union, allowing it to reach and persuade a wider audience than otherwise would have been.

Centre for Liberty Report on CANZUK

Finally, this policy paper will push the limits of concept beyond replacing European Union institutions. Many of the pro-CANZUK articles previously written have focused directly on replacing functions of the European Union. This can be seen through both the appeal to free-trade and free movement, such as Senator Paterson's paper for the *Adam Smith Institute* (Paterson, 2020) and the basis of CANZUK International petition to the British Parliament and change.org (Skinner, 2020). It is most certainly not a criticism that this approach has been taken and the work that has gone into this side of the CANZUK concept is very much creditable and supported. However, this part of the idea has been covered fairly comprehensively and threatens to keep CANZUK as a part of the European Union membership debate, with both being agreements that the United Kingdom had with the European Union. To keep the focus purely on free trade and free movement would be to continue to frame the concept as a direct replacement for the European Union. Therefore, this paper will cover those two aspects of CANZUK as an idea because they are relevant and are needed to present to make this anywhere near a compressive policy paper. but they will not be the main points of this document, which instead will focus on the benefits beyond replacing European Union agreements for the British. That will allow this paper to both be more relevant to the three new kingdoms of CANZUK, unlike European Union debate, and attempt to make CANZUK an idea that goes across party and referendum lines by not focusing on what divides Brexiteers and Remainers.

To that end, this article will be structured as follows. There will be a discussion of the Anglosphere and how there is a common identity to the CANZUK Kingdoms and how this is the basis for both common trust and unity between the citizens, parliaments and governments of the four kingdoms. It will look at what it means to be Australian, British, Canadian and New Zealander and how that is inseparable from broader Anglospheric identity. The second part will cover the case for free trade, followed by the case free movement based upon the shared identity. These two points will be built upon the groundwork of the shared identity, using the trust that is embedded into a shared sense of identity to explain why free trade with regulatory recognition and immigration work considerably better than would normally be the case because of the link of identity. After that, this policy paper will attempt to form the new parts of CANZUK outside the remit of the British European Union membership debate. It will start with how CANZUK, as a common identity and history, can be used as the basis for real, rather than invented, human rights within each kingdom and why the basing of human rights in that shared history is desirable. The rest of the main body of the paper will focus on international policy, as it is where there is the largest scope for CANZUK cooperation. There will be a discussion of the current state of international affairs, how the main democratic and Anglospheric power, the United States of America, is struggling in policy and needs a new force to back it. To that end, this paper will use the consent-based intervention system, argued by Oxford economist Paul Collier (Collier, 2009), as the basis for using the idea of contract and consent to create a viable and affordable foreign policy that is both ambitious and non-expansionist whilst still promoting democracy and human rights internationally. That, along with the shared identity, will be the basis for the final two policy parts. The first will be a sharing of international obligations. This paper will focus on how the United Kingdom's seat on the United Nations Security Council could be used as a CANZUK seat without compromising any of the four kingdoms' independence in the United Nations. The focus on the United Nations is taken as there is a clear path to achieve agreement and as a potential program that could be replicated in other institutions. The final one will be a look at how the nuclear deterrent could be created at the CANZUK level, giving access to legal nuclear weapons to the three new kingdoms and making the nuclear deterrent cost effective.

As stated, the aim of the paper is to take the CANZUK concept out the framing of the British European Union membership debate. That is why there is a focus on international integration, human rights and foreign policy, as these are the ideas that haven't been caught by the Brexit divide. The focus on them is not to argue that they should be enacted first, as free trade is clearly the most immediately beneficial to the citizens of the four kingdoms. The emphasis on the other parts is, instead, as an effort to show where CANZUK could head and how it could be used beyond economic assistance.

Centre for Liberty Report on CANZUK

Anglosphere

The Anglosphere, despite being a new term originating from Neal Stephen's 1995 book The Diamond Age (Stephen, 1995), is a concept that has existed for a couple hundred years. It is an attempt to describe what it is that creates a sense of commonality between the people of the English-speaking world and those closely associated with it. To understand the Anglosphere, knowledge of theories of nationhood is required as the Anglosphere is a category that sometimes encompasses and on other occasions is a nation.

A nation is a difficult concept to define as it is an attempt to describe a phenomenon in human society, rather than create one, and as a result, finding the edges of the concept is challenging because it is an invented category trying to describe human actions. It is for this reason that political scientist Hugh Seton-Watson wrote that he came to 'the conclusion that there is no 'scientific definition' of a nation can be devised' (Seton-Watson,

1977). Therefore, the following on national identity and how it links to the idea of the Anglosphere will not be an attempt to prescribe definitions but instead give a general overview of the sort of meaning that is being intended, even if an exact meaning cannot be created for an invented category for a human idea.

Benedict Anderson, building upon the work already done by Seton-Watson, formalised imagined communities theory. This theory, in Anderson's own words, was based upon the understanding that 'members of even the smallest nation will never know most of their fellow-members, meet them, or even hear of them, yet in the minds of each lives the image of their communion.' (Anderson, 1983) By this, Anderson pointed out that nobody in a nation knows every other member of their nation and as a result, the basis of membership is not the personal knowledge of the other individuals in the nation but instead the perception of them sharing characteristics and loyalties. This characteristic of nations, their basis in perception (which most certainly can be informed by reality), is why Seton-Watson wrote that 'a nation exists when a significant number of people in a community consider themselves to form a nation' (Seton-Watson, 1977). However, for that belief to exist, for people to see 'the image of their communion' (Anderson, 1983), people need to have an idea of what makes them a nation, what they perceive they have in common with their fellow nationals and what makes them different. Those two factors are of vital importance. Perception is based in reality, even if it takes time to react to reality and as a result, for people to perceive that they are in one common group, there needs to be something that links that group together. If there is nothing that links the group, there would be nothing to make the people of a nation feel like they are one nation. Furthermore, if there is a characteristic that unites the nation, by extension it must also be related to what makes the group different. For, if there is not something that makes the group unique, then there is no mechanism to describe it. Two nations that had the same characteristic, deciding who is in which nations would be impossible. They would be, even if not connected by territory, the same national identity. Language requires perceived distinction, otherwise there would be no need for different words. We don't name each individual blade of grass on a field because they are not perceived to be unique, even if each is a different organism. Meanwhile, we differentiate the names of people, because they are each perceived to be unique. If two nations were the same in what made their members who they were, it would be impossible to describe them as different and therefore, no different names could be used for them. As a result, the two characteristics needed for a national identity, at the most basic level, are a perception of there being characteristics that unite the members of the nation and a perception that those characteristics are different to those of other nations.

However, those are not the only characteristics of a national identity, for if they were, any identity would be a national identity. The other side of the national identities is how they relate to politics. Whilst nations are 'pre-political identities' (Scruton, 2006), insofar as what makes a national identity and loyalty an identity is not its political nature, nations take on a political form. Anthony Smith wrote that 'national identity involves some sense of political community' (Smith, 1991). Nations claim the right to governance, the idea of self-determination. This is why there are nation-states, governments based upon the premise that their jurisdiction covers only land which their fellow nationals live upon.

Nation-states come with many advantages. At the high level, a strong national identity in a nation-state makes people more likely to pay their taxes, with better public services as a result (Miguel, 2004), and the country as a whole less prone to civil war (Collier, Hoeffler and Rohner, 2009) due to the increase sense of commonality and desire to help one's own created through national identity. People, due to the belief in rules being made by their own community, also tend to accept election results that don't do their way more readily (Scruton, 2017). This is so extreme a phenomenon, that Hannan argued that 'without a demos, there is no democracy' (Hannan, 2016,

A), without a people, there can be no rule by the people. Beyond that, at the personal level, civility tends to be higher in places where people's sense of 'first person plural' (Scruton, 2014) are national, with trust between people being greater (Barr, 2003) and people more willing to cooperate with those of other races and ethnicities (Blouin and Mukand, 2019).

These advantages are gained through having the people of a country have a sense of commonality with their other citizens which also makes them unique from other countries. It is that which the sense of loyalty and commonality towards others of the same national 'imagined community' (Anderson, 1983) is built upon. That ability to distinguish what one's nationality is and who is a part of it is the foundation of those benefits and without which, those advantages cannot be accessed. With respect to CANZUK and the broader Anglosphere, there is the question of what makes each nation within.

This is where the questions of what unites members of the nation and what makes them unique comes into consideration, as it is incredibly difficult to create such a definition for any of the four kingdoms of CANZUK without including the vast majority of members of the other. There is, in the words of CANZUK International Founder James Skinner, the sense that 'we are virtually the same people with *"only the cover of our passports dividing us"'* (Skinner, 2018, A). This has happened because of the aspects of identity that form the perception of commonality and uniqueness of the CANZUK nations.

The debate around what factors contribute to identity in the Anglosphere is often divided between accusations of racial identity by those who don't identify as a member of one of the CANZUK kingdoms and explanations of an identity based upon beliefs by those who do identify with any of the four kingdoms. Using the example of the United Kingdom, it is a rather odd situation in which people who are not British try to tell the British who they are, which tends to come with a level of arrogance that most people who are British do not appreciate.

There have been a number of books and articles, even in the 21st century, that have attempted to claim that the British are a racial category. Despite their excellent historiography in the first part of their 2019 article, both Bell and Srdjan have written less agreeable articles and books on the Anglosphere, including *The Anglosphere: a genealogy of a racialized identity in international relations* by Srdjan, who argued in that book that the Anglosphere is a part of a 'racialized process' (Srdjan, 2011) and Bell, who focused on the nation as a part 'of the modern capitalist political-economic system' (Bell, 2003) in his article *Mythscapes: Memory, Mythology, and National Identity.* However, by far the worst academic article that discusses identity in the Anglosphere and CANZUK is Mark Ølholm Eaton's 2020 article *'We are all children of the*

Centre for Liberty Report on CANZUK

commonwealth': political myth, metaphor and the transnational commonwealth 'family of nations' in Brexit discourse, who simultaneously complained about the supposed problem of 'rhetoric' (Eaton, 2020) and 'discourse' (Eaton, 2020) whilst accusing those he disagreed with of perpetuating a 'myth' (Eaton, 2020) creating a series of unnecessary new terms to linguistically (rather than logically) undermine the work of pro-CANZUK supporters. Eaton's work is somewhat of a marvel of ridiculousness, with a particular highlight being 'Political communicators in both the public and private realms—politicians, policy-makers and public intellectuals—often closely collaborate in the construction and communication of political narratives, including political myths' (Eaton, 2020). Given how disparaging and vitriolic Eaton is about how people who support CANZUK 'collaborate' (Eaton, 2020), it does beg the question of whether Eaton would rather that all of those whom he happens to not agree with don't work together to achieve what they think will benefit their countries and the world in general. Eaton's apparent surprise and disgust at people who 'collaborate' on ideas he doesn't agree with is almost worth reading for the hilarity of it. Unfortunately, it is an actually published academic article that fits into a trend of content that tries to tell the British, Canadians, Australians and New Zealanders who they are with little reference to who they think they are and how they have historically existed.

Ciarán Reed

It is clear, despite both the best attempts of some in the United States of American, the BNP and those who disagree with CANZUK and the Anglosphere, the identities at hand are not a racial identity. The history of Britain before the adventures in the New World is case enough, with the mixing of different Celtic tribes, Romans, Angles, Saxons, other Germanic tribes, Vikings and Normans for just the invasion-based movement of people, let alone the standard migration outside of conquest that took place means that defining the English, let alone the Welsh, Scottish and Irish combined, as a racial category is absurd. Englishness alone was not even a category of white people, with substantial evidence to prove that of the crew of the Mary Rose, the most flag ship of Henry the VIII's naval fleet (and therefore the most important ship in the Royal Navy in first half of the 16th century) was manned by an English mixed-race crew. Of the ten crewmembers' DNA studied in 2019, 'They said four of the skeletons were of southern European heritage, and one seems to have hailed from Morocco or Algeria' (BBC News, 2019), demonstrating that Englishness has not historically been a racial category, as those from other racial groups were trusted and employable by the English crown in the most important of ships. As a result, it has to have been something else that has united initially the British, with the English as a subset of that, and the Anglosphere as racial unity has not existed for over a thousand years and not as a solely white group for at least 500 years. Ultimately, there was a reason why the vast majority of people in Britain did not see the BNP as a serious option, that being their racialised version of Britishness did not correspond with history or the present reality that voters experienced.

Instead, the Anglosphere has been what Francis Fukuyama termed a 'creedal' (Fukuyama, 2018) and Hannan described as 'civic' (Hannan, 2010). The basis of identity in the Anglosphere has traditionally been a shared set of common values and beliefs, with also a tie to language for vast swathes of the Anglosphere.

Those who identify as members of the four countries of CANZUK tend to emphasise that lack of racial connection between their fellow members of the Anglosphere and instead place emphasis on those common values. One of the best lists on what those values are was provided by Friedrich von Hayek, the Austrian economist who became a British citizen after refusing to work in Nazi controlled regions. Hayek wrote that what made the Anglosphere unique was 'independence, self-reliance, individual initiative and responsibility, the successful reliance on voluntary activity, non-interference with one's neighbours, and the tolerance of the different and queer, respect for custom and tradition, and a healthy suspicion of power and authority.' (Hayek, 1944, p.220) In that list, Hayek identified those beliefs and characteristics which he thought were unique to English speaking territories. These are the values that unite the people of the Anglosphere that were also identified by Hannan (Hannan, 2013) and historian David Starkey (Starkey, 2015). These are not just what people happen to believe, it is the core of the identity. It is what both have traditionally made the Anglopheric people different from others and united them into one collective. It is the fundamental basis of identity, with being Canadian, Australian, British and New Zealander contingent upon believing in these values, which most certainly have not been universal throughout history (Hannan, 2013). It is what distinguished the Anglosphere from the rest of the World. Whilst other countries may have some of these aspects, they are not integral to who they are. For someone who identifies as a part of an Anglospheric nation, these are not just traits of what makes good governance and a healthy society but inseparable parts of their personal identity. To change these would be to literally change the person, to change their identity.

It is from that common set of values that a number of the key institutions of the Anglosphere has evolved. The tolerance inherent within the creedal identity allowed for the development of the concept of a loyal opposition, with parliament being willing to be fairly disparaging of the government (then truly headed by the monarch) on and off since the 13th century at the latest (Jones, 2012) and the trust in the continuity of the Anglospheric community and individual rights that allowed the common law to develop. Both of those institutions, along with other traditions, customs and organisations of the Anglosphere, as especially seen in the CANZUK Kingdoms with the very direct link to their origins that is made, are observable manifestations of that first, creedal, part of the Anglospheric identity.

That is the first part of Angloshperic identity, with the second part being a leaning, even if not wholly, on the English language. There are parts of the Anglosphere, most notably Quebec and parts of Wales, where English is not the dominant language. However, in each case, there is still a strong influence of English-speaking culture on the areas where other languages are spoken.

Despite that, the influence of the English language on the identity, creedal values and culture of the Anglosphere should not be under emphasised. How language informs identity was addressed by the German nationalists of the late 18th and early 19th century. Johann Fitche argued that language informed the ability of people to think. Historic memories and knowledge are passed, within Fitche's understanding, through language. Language, to Fitche, is how knowledge is retained and transmitted and therefore, speaking the same language as forbears is how their knowledge is retained. This was pushed further than just the ability to access history.

Fitche argued that each language was unique, that there could not be a literal translation as each language contains that knowledge inside the words themselves. As a result, a translated idea is not exactly the same set of thoughts as expressed in the original language. This link is why language is a considerably stronger bond of identity than race. In the (somewhat ironically translated) words of Fitche 'It does not matter if ever so many individuals of other race or language are incorporated with the people speaking this language' (Fitche, 1808, p.35) because it is the language that they express their thoughts in and that is what makes people similar. That is why Fitche defended (in that quote) people who were both born into other cultures, linguistic groups or races from the originals of a nation and were then integrated into the nation, arguing it 'does not matter' (Fitche, 1808, p.35) however 'many individuals' (Fitche, 1808, p.35) of them there are. That is because a nation is not a race or where someone is born, it is what a person thinks, informed by their language, which can be learned.

That belief is what transferred across the globe in the Anglosphere. Fitche's other pertinent point for CANZUK from his *Fourth Address to the German Nation* was that 'Man easily makes himself at home under any sky, and the national characteristic, far from being much changed by the place of abode, dominates and changes the latter after its own pattern' (Fitche 1808, p.32). When the

Centre for Liberty Report on CANZUK

Anglosphere was originally settled (including when modern day England was originally settled) the settlers took their ideals of liberty, freedom and limited government with them. The Anglosphere is Anglopsheric because, wherever those who founded Anglospheric countries came from places that had and kept their original creedal identity. The Germanic tribes took it with them to the British Isles and the British carried it with them to the New World. What made them who they were was not changed by their place of residence, the British who settled Canada, Australia and New Zealand didn't suddenly stop being British when they arrived, they carried on as they were. Once those original settlers were added to by people from other non-Anglospheric countries, by merging with the local Anglophone population and speaking English, the newcomers became Angloshperic in thought, as Fitche argued they would.

This is why a large number of countries that were settled by the British have retained large amounts of Britishness as a part of their governance and identity. That can be seen not just with the CANZUK Kingdoms and their clear retained link with the Anglosphere through the monarchy but also the Anglospheric republics, such as the United States of America, India and Ireland. Certainly, in the case of India, the role of the Anglosphere should not be ignored. The rights that have come through the retention of the Anglosphere's common law and democratic values have been retained due to the Anglosphere (Ferguson. 2003. p.369-371) (Hannan. 2013. p.309). That does prompt the question of why it is CANZUK that has gained so much attention and growth rather than a union of all English-speaking countries or the Commonwealth.

This is where the issue of identity comes back into play. The Anglosphere is not one homogenous set of countries, all being the same people in different places. Whilst the identities are clearly linked through language and custom, there is difference, and in some places they are irreconcilable differences, between the Anglospheric countries. A good point of comparison would be with the United States of America. The key difference is twofold. There is the difference of the power of the legislature and the monarchy. The role of the legislature, being reduced in the United States of American compared to the United Kingdom (Bagehot, 1867) and the other CANZUK Kingdoms. The creed that creates the belief in the constitution of the United States of American is very clearly related to the creedal identity of the CANZUK Kingdoms (Hannan, 2010) but is still distinct because of that difference in legislative power and the monarchy. There is a clear demarcation there within the Anglosphere between the Westminster Style Commonwealth Realms and the Anglospheric republics.

Centre for Liberty Report on CANZUK

Then comes the question of why just the CANZUK Kingdoms and not all of the sixteen Commonwealth Realms. It is both a question of consent and commonality. The common accusation is that CANZUK is a 'white man's club' (Geoghegan, 2020), however such complaints both ignore the creedal nature of the identity and come along with general unnecessary nonsense. Geoghegan, in his Guardian article, went on to ask why 'Jamaica and Papua New Guinea are omitted' (Geoghegan, 2020). It is simply the case that those countries don't want to be a part of it. A number of the Caribbean Kingdoms are actively seeking to become republics (BBC News, 2020, A) (Harding, 2012). There is a general trend across large parts of the other Commonwealth Realms away from being kingdoms, which leads to the slightly odd situation where CANZUK critics accuse CANZUK of being 'Empire 2.0' (Geoghegan, 2020) and question why it is not trying to convince countries that very clearly don't want to be a part of CANZUK into it against their consent. If other territories, which meet the branch of Anlgospheric identity that is the Westminster Kingdoms, want to be a part of it, of course there is a place for discussion. However, there is no clear campaign within other Commonwealth Realms to be a part of the CANZUK project and therefore, it would be against the consensual nature of the concept, there is no need to attempt to include them outside of the facetious complaints of someone who wants to tell the Anglosphere that it's racist without appearing to understand or even consider the view of it as a creedal identity. Furthermore, the second problem with this criticism of CANZUK is that it is questionable whether these countries that are cited actually are involved in that sense of identity, even if they still have Her Majesty Queen Elizabeth II as their monarch. Papua New Guinean identity is considerably more complicated than identity in the four CANZUK Kingdoms (Fukuyama, 2011, pp.xii-xiii). The linguistic diversity, with the result of diverse senses of identity, found in the other Commonwealth Realms makes their inclusion in CANZUK significantly more difficult. If the people do not believe they are a part of the identity, it should be down to their self determination whether they join, rather than having it enforced by the constitutional arrangements they live under. This is before the question of the rule of law in other potential members is questioned. Therefore, as stated earlier, if a country can be plausibly included within the group and there is a groundswell of support for membership, then there can be a discussion. However, there is yet to be any clear candidate and therefore, does not need to be addressed.

This leaves the CANZUK Kingdoms separate from the rest of the Anglosphere. Their focus on both the fully functioning Westminster system and monarchy makes them separate from other parts of the Anglosphere.

Centre for Liberty Report on CANZUK

However, how there are some subtle differences from each other. There is the potential question of French cultural influence in Canada but this clearly hasn't got in the way of CANZUK as it has taken most hold as a concept in Canada, being supported by the main opposition party (Conservative Party of Canada, 2018). At that point, the question of what makes each countries' identity is impossible to define without including the members of the other. This is why it is so easy for members of the Anglopshere to integrate in each other's countries (Forsythe. 2013). It seems beyond current understanding to see each of the four CANZUK Kingdoms as being inhabited by different peoples. It very much seems that Fitche was right that both people will carry their national characteristics to a new land and people who then join those areas become like their adopted nation (Fitche, 1808). It appears that they are the same people who just happen to live in different places. If the four kingdoms were territorially contiguous they would be one continuous nation and there would most probably be very reasonable calls for them to be united into one nation-state. However, they are not and therefore it would be problematic through: the impracticability of governing a transcontinental nation-state from one central government; the distance leading to disconnect between the government and parliament to the people, which could create resentment and a lack of accountability; and belief amongst a large number of members of the Anglosphere in the devolution of power to small localised areas of governance.

That idea is from where this paper will head. Looking at the citizens of the CANZUK Kingdoms as the same people who happen to live on different land masses. This paper will look at how that can be used to benefit all four CANZUK Kingdoms through some combined policy decisions. It will attempt to do this both with the principle that all four parliaments should remain supreme and that every single decision must be consented to. These principles will be expanded upon as the paper goes on but are necessary principles to protect the Westminster system that is a heart of the political systems and identity in the CANZUK countries. From those principles and the concept of CANZUK identity links the policy points will be made.

Centre for Liberty Report on CANZUK

Trade

Proposals for free trade agreements between the CANZUK Kingdoms have been one of the areas where the current literature on CANZUK has focused upon rather extensively. This leaves little scope for original work and, as a result, not much more can be achieved through this point other than a summary of work already available. Furthermore, the literature has tended to focus on the mechanisms by which a CANZUK free trade deal could be created. However, the UK government's announcement of an application to join the Comprehensive and Progressive Trans-Pacific Partnership (CPTPP) (DIT and Truss, 2021), which appears (at least in the short term) to be the answer to how a free trade area could be created with the CANZUK Kingdoms. Beyond that, most of the work previously on free trade has been set within the framework of the question of British membership of the European Union. With that now concluded, the question of CANZUK or the European Union is no longer a current debate as the United Kingdom has a trade agreement with the European Union. To dwell too long on free trade would be to place this paper back into the debates of the previous decade of British politics, rather than place it into the context of politics across all four kingdoms in the 2020s. Therefore, for all of those reasons, not too much time will be spent upon this section of the paper.

The economic benefits of CANZUK are, as numerous articles and reports have previously covered, immense, with David Ricardo's theory of comparative advantage (Ricardo, 1817, pp.107-134) being the intellectual bedrock to the benefits of free trade and the explanation of why, in normal circumstances, both sides are better for engaging in trading relations. The benefits from free trade are not based upon something, at least in the first part, to do with the shared culture of the parties involved but are advantageous for any countries on Earth that trades with each other. Ricardo's theory is written to be true for all nations. This is because of the positive impact of specialisation in the amount that is produced in the overall economy of each country involved, increasing economic output, access to goods and prosperity for both sides, even in the situation where one country is more efficient and can produce an absolute amount more of every good and service (Ricardo, 1817, pp.107-134). CANZUK, therefore, should not be seen as an exclusive trading zone because it is of benefit to trade with as many nations as possible. This is why it is somewhat strange that one of the largest criticisms of CANZUK is that 'only a minuscule proportion of the CANZUK nations' trade is with each other' (Roussinos, 2020). As long as even one good or service crosses the border in a more efficient manner, there are still the benefits from free trade due to comparative advantage (Ricardo, 1817, pp.107-134). That criticism of CANZUK only works when CANZUK is framed as an either-or option between it and another trading bloc, but it is not. To frame the debate as such is to both make the debate British-centric and remain within the European Union debate. Now it is clear that the British can engage with the European Union and CANZUK, the complaint doesn't hold valid, as any trade benefit can be added to the existing arrangements the four CANZUK Kingdoms already have. That is why New Zealand Prime Minister Jacinda Ardern called for 'A modern, high quality free trade agreement (FTA) between New Zealand and the UK' (Ardern, 2018). Free trade agreements don't replace each other but complement each other. Therefore, a CANZUK free trade deal, by virtue of being a free trade deal that would not replace any other existing arrangements, would be of economic benefit regardless of what percentage of trade currently transact between the four kingdoms.

Furthermore, it is likely that free trade between the CANZUK Kingdoms would see an increase in the share of trade between the four kingdoms. The link of common law legal systems, language and custom (all addressed above) will make trade considerably easier than with countries with: different legal systems or no stable rule of law; different languages; and different cultural traditions. The similarities between the four kingdoms mean that it will be both easier for the governments to arrange free trade deals with each other and for the people of the four kingdoms to make trades with each other, using common language and understanding, more than it normally is in international trade. These factors, whilst by their nature incalculable, are likely to make such a trade deal more beneficial than would otherwise be the case with such arrangements between countries with as much geographic distance as the CANZUK Kingdoms have.

Once it is accepted that free trade between the CANZUK Kingdoms would be of benefit to all four kingdoms, the next consideration is how such arrangements should be formed. There are three main ways through which these arrangements could be made: individual trade deals between kingdoms; the kingdoms joining existing institutions; and the creation of a separate, new, four-way trade treaty between the four kingdoms.

Centre for Liberty Report on CANZUK

The first of those options has already been explored by the governments of the four kingdoms. There is already a trade agreement between Australia and New Zealand (Australia–New Zealand Closer Economic Relations Trade Agreement {CER]); the United Kingdom and separately both Australia and New Zealand (yet to become full free trade but mutual recognition agreements) (DIT, 2019, A and B); and in the works between the United Kingdom and Canada (DIT, 2020). The individual deals allow for each kingdom's government (at the accountability of their respective parliament) to make decisions on its arrangements with each of the other three kingdoms on an individual basis, thereby allowing more flexibility and tailoring than other options. All four CANZUK Kingdoms have explored these options alongside option two. These individual agreements have provided for better trading relations between the four kingdoms but, by being individual agreements, make it difficult to coordinate and as a result, are less efficient and slower to create than multi-way agreements. This has left the situation where the United Kingdom currently only has a mutual recognition agreement with Australia and New Zealand ((DIT, 2019, A and B) and is yet to conclude an agreement with Canada (DIT, 2020). As a result, whilst these agreements have allowed for continuity during times of change in other trade agreements, they may not be the best solutions for a more comprehensive and long-lasting trading arrangement.

This is why the second option of having the four CANZUK Kingdoms join already existing agreements appears more desirable. Seymour argued that Canada and the United Kingdom should join the CER, alongside the free movement deal between Australia and New Zealand (Seymour, 2019), with free movement being dealt with later in this policy paper. The choice of joining already existing organisations has also been promoted by Hannan (Hannan, 2016, p.162-163 and 167, B) and it appears that this is a route that the United Kingdom's Department for International Trade has chosen to pursue as well, with an application to CPTPP being announced on the 30th of January 2021 (DIT and Truss, 2021). This option comes with two main advantages, those being that there is less need for creating a new legal text and allows the joining kingdom to gain better trading relationships with countries outside of CANZUK. Joining larger bodies than just the CANZUK Kingdoms will give access to more markets for CANZUK based companies, which due to comparative advantage (as explained above) is of benefit to all four kingdoms. CPTPP, as a bloc of 11 counties, if therefore of benefit beyond just CANZUK trade for the United Kingdom to join. Furthermore, the lack of need for a new legal text means that time for creating free trade conditions is significantly reduced, with minor details and interpretations that usually cause delays in trading agreements, makes joining already existing institutions desirable. This means that joining pre-existing arrangements, be it CPTPP or CER, is the quickest way of achieving free trade between the CANZUK Kingdoms.

This is why the third option, creating a new trade agreement, is not the best option of the three. Both the time it would take to create a four kingdom CANZUK trade deal and the lack of need to do so, when the benefits of trade outside of CANZUK as well can be more easily experienced without it, means that there is no need to create such a new treaty. As a result, the blend of the transition arrangements between the individual kingdoms and the joining of pre-existing organisations is the most desirable pathway for the CANZUK Kingdoms to take in creating free trade between the four of them.

Theoretically, option two (joining already existing institutions and arrangements) could be a predecessor to a full CANZUK treaty encompassing all four kingdoms. That would, however, be both unnecessary and potentially overly bureaucratic. Once there are no tariffs and mutual recognition of production, there will be no need for a CANZUK trade agreement. It might be romantically nice to have CANZUK all covered on their own by one treaty but once the main objectives have been achieved, it won't be needed. To attempt to do option two as a placeholder waiting for option three, unless there are fundamental flaws with the arrangement that is entered into, would be to waste the time and resources of civil servants who could be doing much more productive tasks, such as making trade agreements with countries that the kingdoms don't already have arrangements with. To try and go from two to three would create a new legal treaty for companies to understand when there would be a perfectly sufficient set of terms already in place, forcing them through unnecessary bureaucratic work.

The substance of the trade deals that are made is also of significance. This part of the case for free trade in CANZUK is the part that is most contained within the debate on British membership of the European Union. The case is rather sensibly made that CANZUK trade should be based upon mutual recognition. That is where products have to meet the safety requirements of the jurisdiction that they are produced in and assumed to be safe for export as a result regardless of the regulations of the country that they are exported to rather than standardisation or alignment – where the regulations of each country in a trading agreement are aligned or where the products have to conform to the standards of where they are being exported to. This would be a sensible situation for however CANZUK trade agreements are eventually made. This is because of the trust that is established between governments and peoples that share an identity. The governments of each of the four CANZUK Kingdoms know that there is no bad intent towards the others as they are the same people. That means that each government can have faith in the others' checks and safety measures. Furthermore, the lack of regulations in one kingdom directly impacting the others, ensures that there is not the sense amongst the citizens of being ruled by a body far away from them. This will ensure both confidence in the system for citizens and ensures that each parliament is still able to have absolute sovereignty over their kingdom, a necessity in the Westminster System that is a part of the uniqueness of CANZUK.

However, this is often expressed as an alternative to the European Union. Hannan argued in his 2016 book *What Next?* for the 'superiority of mutual product recognition over standardization.' (Hannan, 2016, p.174, B). This was a perfectly valid argument but was expressed in a book about what the United Kingdom should do following its' European Union referendum result and as a contrast to the regulatory alignment procedures of the European Union. This has left this argument about how CANZUK should proceed in creating trading relationships in the debate around the United Kingdom's relationship with the European Union rather than on its own merits. As a result, it would be recommendable that, going into the future, the point on mutual recognition is made without comparison to the European Union, as to do so is to alienate parts of the citizenry of the United Kingdom and to make it a British-centric argument, rather than one based upon CANZUK's own merits. Escaping this situation, given how CANZUK has both been proposed and opposed based upon it being an alternative to the United Kingdom's European Union membership, will require both careful framing by CANZUK supporters and to place more thought (as happens below) into the aspects of CANZUK that are not areas that the European Union integrates on.

What is clear is that, due to comparative advantage theory, the CANZUK Kingdoms having a free trade agreement, however it is formed, would be of benefit to each individual kingdom. Getting free trade between the kingdoms, given the advantages in trade of law, custom and language, will provide a direct improvement in the lives of the citizens of each kingdom. It will lead to an increase in prosperity and jobs. As a result, it is most probably the area in which the broadest amount of benefit will be experienced by the citizens of each kingdom and therefore, is the most important to achieve first. This should not, however, be the end of CANZUK integration, as benefits of cooperating within the shared identity can be experienced through other areas of integration as well.

Centre for Liberty Report on CANZUK

Free Movement

Free movement between the CANZUK Kingdoms has been one of the main policy positions of CANZUK supporters in recent years. This should not be of surprise given that *CANZUK International* was originally founded as *The Commonwealth Freedom of Movement Organisation* (On Think Tanks, 2020). However, as with free trade (as argued above), this point is often made as an aspect of the debate of British membership of the European Union, with it having been posed in the past as a choice between free movement for British citizens in Europe or CANZUK. Since free movement has ended between the United Kingdom and the European Union, this policy paper will focus on CANZUK free movement as a policy in its own right for all four CANZUK Kingdoms, rather than as a British-centric argument wedged into a wider debate about the European Union.

It should first be noted that support for free movement within CANZUK is, in general, not support for unlimited free movement of all citizens regardless of circumstance but instead visaless travel and the right to permanent residence (with whether the kingdom's government wants to record the distinction being to their own discretion) being available to all of good character who are citizens of any of the other CANZUK Kingdoms. One of the mechanisms that has been proposed for it has been for Canada and the United Kingdom to join TTTA, the free movement arrangement between Australia and New Zealand. People with criminal convictions, contagious health issues and those who have ever been deported from any county can be blocked, with permission needed for those involved in racist organisations, convicted of sexual offenses or generally believed to be a potential threat to the kingdom needing a waiver (New Zealand Immigration, 2021, A). Free movement does not and should not mean allowing criminals to cross borders or endanger any of the four kingdoms that they do not originate from. To not have those restrictions would be to allow the movement of dangerous individuals, making it harder for them to be traced. That sensible flexibility already available in the TTTA would be transferred in the event of free movement being achieved through Canada and the United Kingdom joining the arrangement and should be incorporated into a new agreement (whether made directly between the four kingdoms or created through individual treaties between each of the four kingdoms on a one to one basis) to ensure that free movement is: not abused; the security of each kingdom is maintained; and supremacy over borders by the government (acting the wishes of the parliaments) is retained. This would make free movement more flexible to the needs to each government and its respective parliament and help it be agreeable to the citizens of each kingdom, whilst still allowing for anyone capable of making the travel and finding the necessary accommodation who is a citizen of another of the CANZUK Kingdoms to relocate their place of residence with their (if CANZUK citizens as well) family. That, in the context of this policy paper, is what is meant by free movement.

The question of free movement in its own right comes to two main points: whether the individuals immigrating will be of economic benefit and whether they will integrate into the host country. On both fronts, it appears that the CANZUK Kingdoms would be suitable for free movement between them.

The point of the economic compatibility of the four kingdoms has been stressed in various sources over the past few years. CANZUK supporters tend to emphasise how similar the GDP per capita between each kingdom is (Skinner, 2018, A). This is important because of the impact it has on low skilled workers. The debate on the economic impact of immigration is characterised by differencing information due to it probably having different impacts on people with differing economic income (Murray, 2017). Not much observation of political debate across the four kingdoms is needed to gain the clear impression that the population of CANZUK have a preference against immigration into their kingdoms from those place that are of lower economic status. That is mostly due to the pressure people from such countries place on the lowest earners in society. This is why all four kingdoms have their own points-based immigration systems that use economic factors in their metrics (Government of Canada, 2021) (New Zealand Immigration, 2021, B) (Department of Home Affairs, 2021) (Home Office, 2020). The desire to limit low wage workers is embedded within the immigration systems of each kingdom. This threat of low wage labour movement is not one that would be present in a CANZUK free movement situation. That is because of the aforementioned often stressed point of the similarity of economic position in each country. Movement between each kingdom, as a result, would not be low wage workers attempting to find better government support or an improvement in living standards simply by moving. Instead, the benefits of immigration would only be unlockable by doing work. This will limit movement to those who are trying to earn in a different place for social reasons or are deploying a skill that is in short supply. Both ways, the similarity of economic situation between the four CANZUK Kingdoms ensures that the benefit of immigration is created through either integrating in the host kingdom's society and providing a skill benefit to that kingdom. This will ensure that, due to those economic conditions, free movement in CANZUK would not have the negative impacts of people from poorer countries taking low paid work and undercutting local inhabitants' wages. This means that free movement in CANZUK would provide the benefit of flexibility of where to live for citizens of all four countries, without a clear negative economic impact on where people chose to move to.

The second benefit is that of identity. For an immigrant to integrate and feel at home within a host country, they need to feel as if they are a part of the 'imagined community' (Anderson, 1983) of where they have moved to. It is to become a part of the nation that they now reside in. This is significantly easier within CANZUK. That concept (as above) of the CANZUK Kingdoms all being a part of one identity means that integrating is easier as there is no large change of identity. This is probably a factor in why there already has been so much immigration between the four kingdoms. Around 1 million British citizens moved to Australia between 1945 and 1970 (Madden, 2013) and 4.8% of the Australian population were born in the United Kingdom, with it being the most common place of birth of Australian residents other than Australia itself (Australian Government, 2020 [B]). There are also over half a million New Zealand born individuals living in Australia (Australian Government, 2020 [A]). Immigration is also common between the other kingdoms as well. The level of immigration between the four kingdoms, with how difficult it currently is with the points-based visa systems, is impressive and demonstrates that CANZUK citizens feel comfortable moving between kingdoms. This is probably why polling has found that the British rank the four CANZUK Kingdoms as the four countries they have the most positive attitude towards, interestingly ranking the three new kingdoms above their own (Smith, 2020). This comfort between the countries, most probably founded upon that shared identity (making citizens of the other kingdoms seem almost like people from another region of the same country) means that free movement would not be a threat to the culture or identity of each place, with immigrants between the CANZUK Kingdoms integrating into their new host kingdom. Therefore, when combined with the economic factors, free movement in CANZUK would not be of threat to each kingdom and, given how many people already move between the kingdoms, would provide opportunities that citizens are likely to take.

However, free movement in CANZUK, beyond the potential economic and opportunity, has the potential of helping with maintaining national identity. Given (as discussed above) integration is one of the main concerns when it comes to immigration and that integration is helped by having a shared identity, emphasising the commonality of CANZUK citizens should help with the national identities of each kingdom. Identifying what makes someone a part of the national identity (not just the legal concept of citizen) makes it easier to distinguish who is in a part of the nation. Given that common identity of the CANZUK Kingdoms, it is impossible to define a member of one kingdom without including them in the category of the others. Granting free movement would be a recognition of that and help with the emphasising of what makes each nation who they are, as internal immigration within a single nation is usually (outside of exceptional circumstances) legal. Free movement would be, as a result, simply treating all of CANZUK as the single identity group it is.

That strengthening of national identity comes with the benefits (argued above) of better trust within society (Barr, 2003), an increased quality of public services (Miguel, 2004) and a stronger acceptance of law and democratic results (Scruton, 2017). By identifying what makes someone a Canadian, Australia, New Zealander and Brit, there could be greater emphasis placed upon it, making the benefits of being a nation-state more secure. Free movement in CANZUK, as a result, would not just be of economic benefit but could be the start of a revitalisation of the culture, tradition and identity of the four kingdoms.

Free movement between CANZUK could also the help existing migrant population within the four kingdoms. Emphasising the basis of the common identity and making it a part of the policy towards immigration will help each kingdom clarify what makes their populations who they are by showing what makes them unique and united, in other words, what makes them who they are. This should help make a clearer path for those already in the four CANZUK Kingdoms to becoming fully a part of the nation. That should come with benefits beyond the social and personal impact of feeling a part of the country that the individual lives in, which should not be understated in the lives of that that would gain a sense of belonging from it. That spreading of understanding of the collective identity could also help ease ethnic tensions. Douglas Murray argued in his 2017 book *The Madness of the Crowds* that ethnic tensions from other parts of the world can be imported with migrant populations when they do not feel a part of their host society (Murray, 2017). Tensions between different identity groups, such as Muslim and Jewish populations, if they still identify with their non-host nation identity as their 'first person plural' (Scruton, 2014), will exist as long as there is conflict in the place of origin and will bring problems to the CANZUK

Centre for Liberty Report on CANZUK

Kingdoms. Populations, when they do not assume new identities, will continue to hold their traditional values, rivalries and concerns, when they come to a new country. By emphasising how they can all be a part of the Anglospheric identity and having government policies that make the perception of that and what the identity is based upon clear, people can be brought into the 'pre-political loyalty' (Scruton, 2017, p,7) of the Anglospheric 'first person plural' (Scruton, 2014). That would give a loyalty beyond those previous identities that may be in conflict in their place of origin, which may lead to conflict spilling into the CANZUK Kingdoms between ethnic minorities if left unchecked. It would, if it became the 'first person plural' (Scruton, 2014), make a connection and loyalty between competing ethnic groups which should reduce the chance of conflict. As a result, having an immigration policy that has an aspect of it that emphasises who the people of CANZUK are, could help those who have immigrated from outside of CANZUK have a clearer understanding of what makes the Anglosphere, giving a an achievable path to integration, becoming a full member of their new community and giving a loyalty above previous identities that may lead to conflict.

Furthermore, it fits into the traditions of the Anglosphere. The Anglosphere has spread by people deciding to move for a better life and settling with people with the same creedal values. All four kingdoms were founded by people who moved in an attempt to improve their lives. They have settled and been added to since but it is an ancient tradition of the Anglosphere for people seeking a new life to move to a land that, in many cases, they hadn't even seen before, let alone thought about settling. Whilst there are some obvious other examples, such as those forcibly transported to Australia, this is how most people's families ended up in a CANZUK Kingdom. Giving a quick form of free movement between the four CANZUK Kingdoms would be to allow people to carry on that tradition of the Anglosphere in moving for a better life and joining (or creating) communities with the same creedal values and identity.

In sum, free movement within CANZUK comes with economic and social benefits that would usually be associated with internal migration within a single nation due to the shared identity. It would be a recognition of the shared identity and treating CANZUK as a shared nation, rather than separate countries as is done at the moment. It would provide opportunities to the citizens of the four kingdoms and, as a result, improve the lives of those involved.

Rights

CANZUK could also provide benefits to the citizens of the four kingdoms beyond the economic benefit of free trade and the opportunity increase that free movement would provide. One area in which this could be seen in human rights. This is where this paper will start to develop both the desire to move the concept of CANZUK beyond the debate around British membership of the European Union by both taking it an area outside the main public debate during the referendum and moving the discussion on CANZUK to beyond where it has previously been focused. There has been some suggestion that CANZUK could coordinate on international human rights, which to a small extent has already taken place (Judah, 2020). However, this paper will, at this point, focus on how CANZUK could help support human rights within the four kingdoms. This will be argued by emphasising the distinction between 'real' and 'arbitrary' rights as defined by 18th century British Whig Member of

Parliament Edmund Burke (Burke, 1790) and 19th century British Conservative Prime Minister (before he became Prime Minister or the Earl of Beaconsfield) Benjamin Disraeli (Disraeli, 1835). There will also be supporting evidence from modern political writers (Hannan, 2013) and historians (Starkey, 2015) who have also contributed to this debate as well as the last 20th to early 21st century philosopher Roger Scruton. It will end with a discussion of how the institutions of the four kingdoms, including parliament and the monarchy, are involved in human rights and what practical policy positions should be deployed to preserve human rights.

Disraeli examined the distinction between the 'abstract' and the 'real', writing that 'to form political institutions on abstract principles of theoretic science' (Disraeli, 1835, p.15), in other words to think, invent or create rights through thought are distinct from rights developed through 'permitting them to spring from the course of events' (Disraeli, 1835, p.15), as happens with 'real' rights, which are discovered through the process of history based upon principles that call to previous situations and resolutions. The main difference is that 'abstract' rights are argued for and written without claiming that they are descended from a historical source, whilst 'real' rights are rights that are asserted based upon their previous existence which has been inherited. 'Real' rights are passed on, in the words of Burke, 'in the same manner in which we transfer our property' (Burke, 1790, p.120) after we die.

The distinction between 'real' and 'arbitrary' rights was brought most starkly to light during and in the aftermath of the French Revolution. This was not the genesis of the distinction but was when, given the attempt at creating a new set of rights in France, when the concepts became the subject of popular debate. A lot of the groundwork for the debate was based upon the previous work of Sir Edward Coke, the author of the 1628 petition of rights, and great defender of common law against Stuart tyranny (Encyclopaedia Britannica, 2021). Both Burke (Burke, 1790, p,117) and Disraeli (Disraeli, 1835, p.21) pointed out in their work that Coke was the inspiration for their arguments, with Hannan also pointing out his inspiration from Coke (Hannan, 2013, pp.113-114) as well. However, the need to create the full distinction between the two types of rights only became fully pertinent during the French Revolution, as Coke's defence was arguing in reference to the need to preserve already existing rights, rather than engaging in a debate about the superiority of traditional 'real' rights compared to than new 'arbitrary' rights. That debate, on the source of rights, is the necessary one to have in the 21st century, especially when compared to limiting the rights of the Crown compared to parliament, and therefore, Burke and Disraeli's writings are the more useful today, even though they are reliant on Coke's original work, because they are dealing with the issue through a debate closer framed to the context of today.

The discussion of rights today often takes the form of the discussion of human rights. However, the stating of human rights does not mean that human rights as a concept reflects reality. A majority of the global population today do not have access to or experience what we would deem in the democratic world to be human rights. Every populated continent has a tyrannical, brutal dictatorship that violates the United Nations Fundamental Charter on Human Rights. It is also not just small, insignificant locations that are impacted as well, Russia, China and Iran, crucial powers in the regions they chose to engage, both violate what are commonly seen as human rights in their own territory and support such abominations in other countries. Human rights, regardless of what would be the ideal from a democratic point of view, are not experienced by a majority of humanity, either in history or today.

Therefore, there needs to be an alternative source of human rights than the international treaties on the matter, as to not have one would provide all people democratic countries the same source of protection for their human rights as those who live in the Democratic Peoples' Republic of Korea, something that would most certainly not be desired. This creates the need for a source for human rights outside of the international treaties, as they do not provide, in and of themselves, a sufficient source to originate meaningfully the basic rights of individuals.

That is the point from which the distinction between 'abstract' and 'real' rights starts, with the need to base and have a source for human rights. One attempt at this has been what was described by Burke and Disraeli as creating 'abstract' rights. 'Abstract' was used by them in the context of the rights proclaimed by the French revolutionaries of the 1789 revolution (Burke, 1790) but has the same basis as other proclaimed rights today. The revolutionaries, and supporters of their revolution, attempted to declare a set of rights for themselves. These rights tended to be based upon previous theoretical writings. However, the source of the rights was the declaration itself. It was not grounded in any certain concept but instead in the views and theories of the people involved in their creations. This is the difference, to Disraeli, between 'inheritance' (Disraeli, 1835, p.21) and 'abstract' (Disraeli, 1835, p.28) rights. The attempt to proclaim was simply an opinion. These rights may have been well reasoned but they only exist through argument. This leaves the rights of citizens in countries that have 'abstract' rights, rights proclaimed by the government or through argument, vulnerable to the removal of human rights. This is for three main reasons: the power of the government (when involved in declarations); the power of physical force to overthrow the rights; and the threat to them by changes in opinion.

The first point on 'abstract' rights is, in the case where it is granted by either the government or legislature, it would remain within the power of the authority that declared or approved such rights to take those same rights away. If an institution, however it is constituted, is capable of deciding what rights citizens have, it is implied that the said organisation is both the declarer and custodian of those rights. In that situation, the organisation in charge has the implied power to remove the rights in question. Even if they declare that they do not have such power, that is simply just a set of words without meaning in reality as if that organisation has the power to decide what is a right, they could only have the legitimacy to do so if the rights are derived from another source (which they cannot be unless they are based in history [as explained below]) or have to have the power to remove the rights. What the government or legislature can create, it can repeal. This has implications for the governance in law-based societies, such as those in CANZUK. For CANZUK, it means that the governments or parliaments of the four kingdoms cannot simply declare rights across the kingdom, as to do so would also be to give them power to take said rights away. In declaring rights they necessarily would only exist as long as the governments and parliaments wished for them to exist. Therefore, within the CANZUK Kingdoms, it would be expedient to have a different source of human rights than declarations from parliament or the government and purely legislatively written rights.

The second point on 'abstract' rights, as defined and explained by Burke and Disraeli, is that they are subject to change through violence. This point comes from two fronts, those being: how violence often establishes 'abstract' rights; and how 'abstract' rights can be removed through violence regardless of if that was its origin. The creation of 'abstract' rights tends to come from violence. Whether it was the violence of the French revolution, Russian revolution or Second World War, most 'abstract' claims to rights have their derivation in violence. As a result, it is violence that can remove them because, once again, a mechanism by which rights can be created is also a mechanism through which those same rights can be removed. The creation of new rights through violence, as a result, would leave rights at the mercy of who is capable of the greatest brutality, rather than have them as unremovable guarantees of liberty, security and decency. It would turn rights, and by extension the constitution, from a set of deliberations and historic precedents to a series of civil wars. It would make military strength and the ability to kill opponents the main mechanism through which rights can be asserted and power obtained. This is not hyperbole, especially given the number of revolutions, revolts, violent protests and coup d'état attempts that have taken place in France since 1790, with violent protests, with violent clashes over the rights and freedoms of French citizens to the police taking place as recently as December 2020 (BBC News, 2020, B). This was noted by Burke who pointed out that supporters of such rights 'almost always sophistically confounded ['abstract' rights] with their power.' (Burke, 1790, p.153) By this, even democratically agreed rights are, even when placed within the national context required for accepting democracy (Scruton, 2017), an expression of which side has physically the most power, highest number of people on their side (and by extension would more plausibly win in a war). The second part on violence is that even if 'abstract' rights. If a right is simply argued as being good or just, that does not necessarily confer legitimacy in enacting them within their own creation or by the people who support them. For an 'abstract' right to be implemented – unless the right is an inherited 'real' right (as argued below), and therefore does not need creating in an 'abstract' argument, or is just an opinion (also argued below) and therefore changeable very quickly – it needs to be able to defend from violence, as it is not inherent to the people or territory. The claim to legitimacy, if it is merely something believed to be good for society or desirably, of implementation without a source external to itself is the same as the claim to legitimacy of any violent force that chooses to overrun it for any reason (or lack of one) it chooses. That goes too for institutions that claim to have the power to declare or enforce rights, with the legitimacy of such institutions when not based in tradition. Ultimately, that ability of people to agree to 'abstract' rights (which is purely the opinion of those with the ability to deploy force) or gain them through the violent suppression of those who disagree implies the means by which to remove that 'abstract' system of rights is through their own violence. As a result, an 'abstract' right can be removed by violence as it does not, by definition, come from a definable factual source and therefore to be implemented, it must be enforced by a physical power and its claim to existence comes through who can control the government, something that is violently asserted (outside of tradition as described below) and therefore is susceptible to violence. As a result, 'abstract' rights should not be the source of rights due to their need to be either violently emplaced or risk being violently overthrown without being illegitimate. As Scruton put it, 'Rights do not come into existence through merely because they are declared. They come into existence because they can be enforced.' (Scruton, 2006, p.20) Unfortunately, without a factual claim, rather than opinion-based claim, to legitimacy, that enforcement inevitably, in the final analysis, is through violence.

The final point on abstract rights is that they are reversible by one change in opinion or argument. However eloquently someone's argument for the creation of an 'abstract' right is, however uncontroversial or self-evident it is claimed to be, it is just an opinion. If it is not based upon precedent or historic events, someone has to have created them as a thought, a choice, a belief in the present, rather than the right having always existed. Even if an 'abstract' right that has not previously been asserted is claimed to be derived from God, it requires the individual who claims the right to have: the opinion of belief in God; the opinion of the creation of that right being God's will; and the opinion that they are in a position to legitimately proclaim and enforce God's will. This means that, in all circumstances, other than rights which are inherited from a source beyond recorded history, 'abstract' rights are simply just the opinions of their authors and implementers. As a result, 'abstract' rights only exist for so long as they are held in the opinions of certain people. That leaves rights precarious due to it only taking those in power to change their opinion for the right to be lost, as those in power, if they are the ones to create and enforce the right, can take it away (as described above). Furthermore, it would leave the right (if the holders of the right do not claim a legitimacy to rule from a previous source) capable of being declared illegitimate by simply anyone changing their opinion. Even if those in power don't change their opinion, it would still leave the right illegitimate in the eyes of anyone who can create a case against it, which if the source of that power only claims legitimacy by 'abstract' opinion, is not a safe place for rights to be stored. It simply takes one argument, however badly it is constructed, however unreasonable it is, to delegitimise an 'abstract' right, if made by a person in power, or by anyone if the rights are enforced by an institution where the power is granted by 'abstract' concepts.

For those reasons, human rights should not be based on 'abstract' ideals, as to do so is to make them insecure, removable at a whim. This is why rights should be based on 'real' historic claims. This is especially the case for the CANZUK Kingdoms given the strength of the 'real' rights claims available through the shared identity.

Rights which are derived from history have a number of significant advantages over rights which are not. They are impossible to completely remove (even if at times they are suspended), they have a grounding outside of mere opinion and can be claimed by all who are capable of linking themselves to the inheritance of the right, making them achievable even against violence, power and tyranny which may wish to remove them.

The historical claim to 'real' rights is the source of their irremovable status. The traditional rights that the Anglosphere, especially the CANZUK Kingdoms, inherit have been ever-permanent features of the existence of the common identity, inseparable from what it means to be Canadian, Australian, New Zealander or British. The rights that are claimed through this fashion can be traced back to before recorded history. This can best be explained through looking at key times when the rights of the Anglosphere (wherever they inhabited) were asserted. Going backwards through the chronology, the 1688 Glorious Revolution was one of the most recent incidents where rights needed to be asserted, an event which both Disraeli and Burke addressed. Burke argued that the Glorious Revolution, and the subsequent Bill of Rights and Claim of Rights 1688/1689 (Clarke, 2015), was 'to derive all we possess as *an inheritance from our forefathers*' (Burke, 1790, p,117). The Glorious Revolution saw the replacement of King James II / VII by King William II / III and Queen Mary II and reassertion of rights against the alleged tyranny of King James II / VII. Those who implemented both actions were clear, and subsequent analysis has been equally clear, did not create new rights. That was the focus of Burke's argument, with those acting at the time instead reasserting *'an inheritance from our forefathers'* for the bill that is still, in parts, enforced not just in the United Kingdom (Gay and Maer, 2009, p.4-5) but also in Australia (Law Reform Commission of Western Australia, 2002, p.201), Canada (Locke, 1989, p.540) and New Zealand (New Zealand Government,

2015). That point was agreed to, centuries later, by Scruton, who argued that it was 'merely rehearsing established procedures of the common law, and re-affirming them against recent abuses.' (Scruton, 2006, p.20) The Bill of Rights claimed to be reinstating the rights that had been inherited from the Magna Carta. It was not, according to Burke and Disraeli, the creation of new rights but the continuation of old. This claim to previous authority was also present at the most infamous expression of rights in Anglospheric history, Magna Carta. Whilst the original 1215 agreement ended up being superseded in the following years by the 1217 and 1225 revisions (Starkey, 2015), with the 1225 one being 'far more important' by making Magna Carta 'a symbolic statement of political principle' (Jones, 2012, p.227), Magna Carta's origin and claim to legitimacy was founded with 'real' rather than 'abstract' rights. Disraeli wrote about the barons who forced Magna Carta's creation, arguing that 'They did not act upon abstract principles' but instead 'acted upon positive conventional right.' (Disraeli, 1835, pp.18-19) The barons, ultimately, were claiming the rights that they, as Englishmen, had inherited from the Anglo-Saxons. These were the same rights that settlers carried with them to the three new kingdoms as well (Hannan, 2013, pp.283-284). These rights, by being traced back to the Saxons (even before they arrived in the British Isles) means that these rights are traceable to before written records. They have, for all intents and purposes, always existed, for time immemorial, rather than being created as an 'abstract' concept or opinion. These 'real' rights are inherited facts, passed from national generation to national generation.

The question becomes who inherits these rights, as they are evidently (as argued above) not accessed by the entirety of humanity, instead just those who can claim them from the Saxons. The answer is not a biological descent. The Anglosphere that has spawned from the Anglo-Saxons isn't one continuous biological unit but instead a series of beliefs, a creedal and civic identity. It is inherent within that identity that rights are passed. Anyone who assimilates into the Anglosphere is a part of that inheritance, as they are the same people (defined by how each Anglospheric identity is defined) as those who previously had the rights, the same identity. That works in reverse as well, with those who may be biologically descended from the Anglo-Saxons capable of leaving the Anglosphere through changes in their beliefs and location. This is also not just theoretical hope but how it has been applied. The two main defenders of 'real' rights during and after the French revolution in the English language, Burke and Disraeli, both were not racially linked to the Anglo-Saxons, Burke being an Irishman born in Dublin, probably secretly a Catholic, and Disraeli, whose family was Jewish. They both easily claimed their inheritance as British because that identity is not a racial one and the 'real' rights are passed through national generations (something Burke focused on heavily, with the link between generation of duty and rights in a nation being a central theme of *Reflections on the Revolution in France*), not familial. That is why 'Britons in New Zealand were keen to assimilate Maoris fully into local social and political structures.' (Hannan, 2013, p.283). They took the same concept, as part of the Anglosphere, with them to the island that are now New Zealand. That attempt at assimilation is in contract to how other European empires functioned, 'The political culture and common law heritage of New Zealand's settlers made it unthinkable for Maoris to be placed into a separate legal category' (Hannan, 2013, p.284). The same logic was why slavery has (as shown by the Somerset case) been banned in the British Isle since the Viking colonisers lost control and England's had a continuous legal system (Hannan, 2013, 284-285). The way that both the United Kingdom and the three new CANZUK Kingdoms have managed to assimilate other races into their national identity is both testament to the strength of the creedal identity of the Anglosphere and how the inheritance of 'real' rights is inherited. By pushing this narrative in CANZUK, that being the link between identity and inherited rights, this explanation of the existence of rights will be further maintained as the identity and inheritance is made clearer.

Once it has been accepted that 'real' rights are distinct from 'abstract' rights due to their inheritance and lack of creation, having essentially always existed, there comes a number of crucial benefits, which CANZUK could help emphasise, those being: the irremovable nature of them; their ability to transcend current trends; and their superiority of their value.

The irremovable nature of them is the most important aspect of 'real' rights and why it is imperative that they are how we base rights in the CANZUK Kingdoms rather than in 'abstract' concepts. The issue of the permanence of rights that are not based in history (addressed above) is solved through having rights that are traceable back to before recorded history. On a surface level analysis, it does not take much effort to demonstrate that the rights experienced today within a nation are reliant upon that nation's history. The reason why human rights are not observed in China is because of the history of the Chinese Civil War and the Communist Party of China having not been overthrown. By the same token, the reason why there are observable rights in the Czech Republic is because they managed to overthrow the communist dictatorship imposed upon them. That is indisputable. However, the link between 'real' rights and history runs considerably deeper. One of the problems (argued above) with 'abstract' rights, rights created through a system of logical thought that are then imposed through either violent force of the government or a violent revolution against the government, is their lack of inherent legitimacy. No organisation can claim, through 'abstract' rights, legitimacy beyond what is simply just an opinion. 'Real' rights circumvent this problem by not being purely an opinion but by being a historical fact. In situating 'real' rights beyond historical record, the Anglo-Saxon rights, which have been inherited through the creedal identity of Anglosphere by the citizens of the CANZUK Kingdoms, are not opinions but the only known reality. As a result, the question of legitimacy comes down to it having always been, a bit like how the Witan, which through a number of guises evolved into the parliaments we have today, and the monarchy, which most probably started as lords in modern day northern Germany – with the medieval English kings emphasising their right to the throne through St Edward the Confessor on many occasions (Jones, 2012, pp.234-236, 241, 266, 298, 363, 559, 562) (Mortimer, 2007, pp.35, 59,194, 219, 269, 348) and some 'Like Henry I [and Henry III}... knitting his own rule into the ancient Saxon lineage, celebrating its English origins, not just its Norman and Plantagenet sophistication.' (Jones, 2012, p.247) – being facts of history that have always existed. That removal of human rights from opinion and placing it into fact means that they cannot be removed through one argument, one lost battle. Whilst at times, including at the time of writing under Covid-19 lockdown restrictions, they can be suspended, they are always the inherited right of each citizen of a CANZUK Kingdom by virtue of their Anglospheric identity and can be asserted without the need to defend whether the rights are good or not because they always have been. It is not like money which can be traded away as they are concepts and principles. As a result, the claim to them is permanent, even when someone attempts to remove them, and they do not require violence to be claimed as legitimate due to how they have always existed and are historical facts, not opinions. It is simply a fact that Anlgospheric people have a right to not be arbitrarily imprisoned. The irremovable nature of 'real' rights, rather than 'abstract' rights makes them preferable.

The rest is a bonus beyond the unchangeable justification for them, as to make how 'real' rights are better the main focus of their justification would be to turn them back into the 'abstract' opinions that they are contrasted against. The bonus of 'real' rights comes with how 'real' rights avoid falling into the fads of the day. Each age has a series of beliefs that seem odd to future generations. A good example would be previous generations views on race and feudalism. Each generation has various concepts and ideas that are, in retrospect, fairly appalling. Whilst some have attempted to figure out what our generation's ones are (Murray, 2019), inherited rights do some of the work to ensure that the overriding legal principle of rights are not overwhelmed. 'Abstract' rights tend to be 'principles which the next age may have rejected' (Disraeli, 1835, p.19) but 'real' rights have already been through the process. The historic nature of them means that to have survived to this stage 'real' rights have been interpreted and pushed by literally thousands of years of political, social and cultural thinking. This means that instead of being the fad concepts of one age, they are principles that can transcend time periods. That means that they are more refined and have, through the process of being removed of the prejudices of the proceeding generations to make it to us now, fewer time period fads within them than 'abstract' rights, leaving them better thought through. As a result, they are more effective in protecting what truly matters, rather than what the current time thinks matters but might, in hindsight, be misguided. This makes them superior in the protection they cover as they protect what is necessary and truly desirable across the ages, rather than reinforcing potential negatives of the thinking of the time that they were implemented. Burke noted that without that wisdom of time the governance of a nation 'would become little better than flies in the summer.' (Burke, 1790, p.192)

Ciarán Reed

Ensuring rights are good is of the utmost importance because of what rights are. Rights, whilst can be defined in many different ways, one perspective that can be taken is that they are when one person's consent is given precedence over another's and democratic choice can be overruled by the consent, or lack thereof, of one other person. A democracy should not be able to vote to imprison someone arbitrarily, despite how many people vote for it. By the same token, a right to appeal allows an individual's consent to challenge a decision to happen regardless of whether who the appeal is against or what body is appealed to wants or consents to that appeal. As a result, rights, by virtue of them being the situations where democracy and consent of one group can be overruled must be taken seriously because they are the areas in which tensions between the values that are held in the Anglosphere between protecting the individual and having parliamentary accountability with the rule of law can come into conflict. To have the rights taken seriously and having rights tested over thousands of years to make them clear and timeless in their nature rather than potentially just a misjudged opinion that the future will see as at best ridiculous or at worse inhumane, is the basis of that bonus benefit of 'real' rights over the possible flaws of any 'abstract' rights.

It should be stressed that 'real' rights being better than 'abstract' rights is just a happy accident, as if it was just that which made them more legitimate, they would just be 'abstract' principles as them being better is an opinion, meaning that they would be no longer 'real' rights, just old opinion 'abstract' rights. It is therefore not that they are better which makes 'real' rights worth having and emphasising in CANZUK but that irremovable aspect inherent to their nature which is important, with the bonus of them being decent being just that, a bonus, not the justification.

In the context of CANZUK, given the clear link to the inherited rights from before recorded history that can be asserted, emphasising that link as the basis of all rights claims (rather than opinions of what policy should be) is the safest way of ensuring that the government does not encroach on rights. All four kingdoms have their justification and claim to the inherited 'real' rights linked through history. The ability of these rights to move geographic location (as they did initially from continental Europe outside of the Roman Empire to the British Empire) and the basis of them in national identity (not familial descent like possessions) is equal across CANZUK and each kingdom's claim is linked to the other three. Therefore, explaining this and basing human rights understanding (not enforcement, as each kingdom's courts and parliaments should be independent to maintain the Westminster system each kingdom is reliant upon) at the CANZUK level is desirable because all four kingdom's links are interconnected. Therefore, cooperation between human rights organisations between the four kingdoms is desirable in protecting human rights.

That is also true for the links to the monarchy and the defence of historic institutions. The historically based justification for the existence of human rights, outside of the scope of opinion and 'abstract principles of theoretic science' (Disraeli, 1835, p,15) is the same justification of the existence of the monarchy and parliament. Anglospheric republics, such as the United States of America and India (Hannan, 2013, pp.290-301), will have to find their own justifications and links (which is perfectly plausible to create given how Anglospheric they still are as nations), but the CANZUK Kingdoms justification for having rights and liberties is inextricably linked to monarchy and parliament. To believe that the monarchy can legitimately be subject to a referendum is to turn the history that created it into something that does not carry with it inherent value. That undermining of history undermines the 'real' human rights and parliaments that go with it. Like the human rights, at times the monarchy can be suspended (such as under Cromwell) and in exceptional circumstances removed to protect the inherited rights, sometimes through replacement by a different monarch – as happened to create the reigns of Edward III, Henry IV, Edward IV,

Centre for Liberty Report on CANZUK

Henry VII and William III and Mary II – or completely abolished all together but only when the monarchy is infringes upon those inherited rights – as happened to the United States of America and to the broad Anglosphere during the dictatorship of Oliver Cromwell. It is only when done in the protection of those inherited rights that the monarch can be replaced by another or abolished. It must, and is, always done within the spirit of carrying on the inheritance, which was why Burke argued that the Glorious Revolution, the last time a sitting monarch was removed against their will, was done 'to derive all we possess as *an inheritance from our forefathers*' (Burke, 1790, p.117).

Whilst there has been a referendum on the monarchy in Australia in 1999, the success in keeping the monarchy is not why the monarchy exists and the monarchy should not be put to referendum. To make the inheritance of the Anglosphere, with all that comes with it, into an 'abstract' opinion decided at the polls, such as who should be the local MP, is to condemn the existence of human rights and democracy in CANZUK. It would turn the entirety of inheritance into an 'abstract' opinion, leaving democracy and human rights in CANZUK with the same level of protection as 'abstract' rights globally. The inherent legitimacy of traditions from before written history is enough, with the baggage of benefit that comes with it, to make the monarchy, human rights and parliament beyond pure opinion and therefore, any referendum on any of the issues is inherently illegitimate and would threaten all that is decent in our politics. This threat was recognised by Burke who wrote that 'We have an inheritable crown; an inheritable peerage; and an house of commons and a people inheriting privileges, franchises, and liberties, from a long line of ancestors.' (Burke, 1790, p.120) All of these exist in some capacity today (even if reformed) and are linked through having the same source of legitimacy, inheritance, as Burke recognised. To delegitimise or even turn into something based upon opinion just one of them is to ruin the legitimacy of all. To pick which ones are inherited it to have an opinion of which ones are desirable and only continuing the parts of the historical inheritance of the Anglosphere that are preferred through 'abstract' thought. Therefore, each CANZUK Kingdom should maintain the crown in protection of human rights and parliamentary democracy and actively do so in the other three kingdoms as to not do so would be to undermine the inheritance of the all.

Furthermore, the benefit of not being constrained by the fads of the day should also be accessed. To achieve that, efforts to create a written constitution in the United Kingdom should be rejected, as it would both override the uncodified tradition that keeps liberty 'real' in the United Kingdom, making the constitution 'abstract' from that 'real' basis, and would entrench the fads of today, rather than letting the historical process protect rights in the more nuanced and successful way. The three new kingdoms needed written constitutions as the institutions of state, whilst successors to those in the British Isles, required a clearly defined set of rules to exist in a functional manner, but are still traces from what was in the British Isles. That link to the uncodified start should be emphasised in debate as the justification for the existence of the structures of the state in the new kingdoms and should be recognised as the basis of constitutions rather than the written form, which is just an expression of it. More broadly, those in all four CANZUK Kingdoms, except in exceptional circumstances (as happened in 1215 and 1689) where rights need to be restated to the Crown, should avoid codifying human rights as to do so would be to place precedent on the newly written rights rather than their original 'real' form, and in doing so make them subject to debate, rather than as a fact of history, which would undermine their legitimacy and longevity.

CANZUK offers the opportunity to re-emphasise the link of identity between the four kingdoms and in doing so, could help secure the rights and liberties that comes with the identity. Once that is recognised, the inseparable link of rights in one CANZUK Kingdom from the other, human rights organisations should cooperate on rights claims to ensure that they are upheld across the entirety of CANZUK. At the policy level, the inherited nature of the rights should be recognised through also supporting the same claim to legitimacy in other areas. The most obvious example of this is that referendums on the monarchy should not just be opposed through campaigning in hypothetical future referendums for keeping the monarchy but should rejected as an illegitimate means of removing the monarchy as it does not derive its legitimacy from opinion but by being a fact of history. To legitimise referendums on the monarchy is to question the facts of history in their present form, which would undermine the justification for the Anglospheric rights of the four kingdoms. To fail to reject such suggestions so would be to reject CANZUK's Anglospheric inheritance, including the rights we enjoy as a result.

International Problems

The rest of this policy paper will be focused on how CANZUK can act outwards, having looked at the internal benefits for the four kingdoms through free trade, immigration and rights protection. However, it is not just internal affairs which could be helped by further cooperation between the CANZUK Kingdoms, foreign policy and military matters are also fields which could be greatly improved by operating at the CANZUK level. As with the previous parts of this policy paper, there will be a discussion of the areas in which there can be an impact at the CANZUK level, with the conclusions being the policies which could be implemented as a result of the preceding discussion.

There are two main problems which CANZUK could help solve. CANZUK has the ability to help promote a new, consent-based approach to the promotion of democracy and be the catalyst to reform in international organisations, such as the United Nations. What is clear is that, at the current rate, there is a need for a new approach to international relations given the failure of democracy to spread beyond the fall of the communist blocs, despite predictions (Fukuyama, 1992), and the growth of tyrannical power, with the expansion of Russia, China and Iran.

Francis Fukuyama has since rescinded upon his prediction of the global spread of democracy (Fukuyama, 2018, pp.xii-xvi), arguing it through the concept of political decay (Fukuyama, 2011) (Fukuyama, 2014). However, *The End of History and the Last Man*'s positive outlook (at least until Part V *The Last Man* (Fukuyama, 1992)) demonstrates the optimism and worldview that should be desired by all who value freedom. The want for the spread of democracy is a desire that should not be dropped because the end of the Cold War did not lead to the universalisation of democracy that was hoped for. CANZUK most certainly will not lead to the end of history or the universalisation of democracy but it is worth looking at the theory for how badly democratic foreign policy has been since the fall of the Berlin Wall in 1989 as the basis from which to explore whether CANZUK can help promote liberty and democracy.

Fukuyama predicted the end of the totalitarian communist control of Eastern Europe in a lecture in

Centre for Liberty Report on CANZUK

February 1989 (Atlas, 1989), writing on the matter in the summer edition of *The National Interest* later that year (Fukuyama, 1989) and publishing his full book in 1992 (Fukuyama, 1992). The initial lecture and subsequent writings are marvels of academic thought. This policy paper will not expand upon the concept of the themotic desire for recognition as it is not linked to CANZUK but it is an example of one the many great concepts contained within Fukuyama's work that has been ignored since by the inaccuracy of the headline. Instead, what will be focused on is the hope for a better world and a democratic order. Fukuyama's predictions in the lecture came true so quickly that he couldn't write the book in time to be realised before the Warsaw Pact communist governments collapsed. That left the United States of America as the only super power left on the globe and the hope was that democracy would therefore spread beyond the already astonishing gains made in Europe.

Inherent within this worldview was democracy being a desirable form of government. This is something that the freedom supporting Anglosphere should have no problem with and is most certainly still the belief today. It was, unfortunately, in the pursuit of that agenda that the first of the major problems that CANZUK could address in international politics came about. That being how democracy is spread to parts of the world that don't have it.

The assumption within *The End of History and the Last Man* was that this would happen naturally, that countries would move towards democracy as their present systems of government flaws become more obvious (Fukuyama, 1992, pp.13-51). This, to begin with, seemed very much to happen by itself, with Eastern Europe. However, momentum slowed, Tiananmen Square showed that the desire for change amongst some in a country was not enough to create the democratic change.

The main change took place following the September the 11th 2001 attacks in New York and the subsequent invasions of Afghanistan and Iraq. It has since become very clear that the initial invasion of Iraq was not done under the most admirable of circumstances (Greenstock, 2016). In the years following those two initial invasions, the desire to spread democracy has significantly decreased to the point at which the belief in the values of democratic society have been significantly questioned by both politicians (Murray, 2017) and by those in democratic societies themselves (Luce, 2017). This has, over the past decade especially, allowed anti-democratic forces to grow in power, with China (through its increased power in Hong Kong, online and in the South China Sea), the Russian Federation (through the invasion of Georgia in 2008, 2014 annexation of Crimea and growth in internet presence) and Iran (through its terrorist and militia growth of military power) to gain influence.

Centre for Liberty Report on CANZUK

Furthermore, opportunities to spread democracy during the 21st century have failed. The most obvious example of such was the Arab Spring, with the vast majority of countries failing to become democratic afterwards. This policy paper is not the place to compare the 1989 revolutions with the Arab Spring but comparisons with 1848 (Fukuyama, 2014, pp.427-435) have already been made, given the failure of both sets of regional revolts. What can be pointed out whilst keeping to the topic of CANZUK was the success in converting a large number of the 1989 revolutionary territories into nation-state democracies compared to the Arab Spring. Between the letting of tyrannies to grow in power and the failure to create new democracies out of revolutions, the democratic world has failed. Whilst successive administrations in the United States of America have failed – Republicans overseeing the invasion of Iraq and the fall of liberty in Hong Kong, Democrats allowing the Arab Spring to fail and Crimea to be annexed under their stewardship – it cannot be the sole responsibility of the United States of America to defend the beliefs of the Anglosphere, let along the whole democratic world.

The inherent benefits of democratic control, the benefits of the accountability it produces (Fukuyama, 2011, pp.321-434) and the genuinely liberating benefit of democracy, something that the Anglosphere (potentially due to the English language) is unusually disposed to supporting (Hannan, 2013, pp.25-33) should be at the heart of foreign policy for the CANZUK Kingdoms. That strong attraction to democracy and away from extremism that is so inherent within the language, culture and identity of the Anglosphere (Hannan, 2013, pp.25-33) that it should be the basis upon which foreign policy is built if it is to reflect who the CANZUK citizens are as people, their beliefs and moral convictions.

To achieve that, it should not be the aim of CANZUK to replace the United States of America as the leading democratic super power. The United States is a key ally of all four CANZUK Kingdoms in military, security and intelligence matters not because of its power but because, on foreign policy, our Anlgospheric beliefs align. The desire to support other democracies, such as Japan and the Republic of Korea, comes from the same source. CANZUK should not be seen as a threat to the United States of America because to become that is to undermine what is and, for as long as they are Anglospheric, will always be our shared foreign policy objectives. CANZUK should be aiming to provide a second democratic global power alongside the United States. Whilst claims of the ability to make CANZUK into a super power tend to come with articles that push the limits of the idea of CANZUK, with Robertson claiming CANZUK could be a super power in the same articles that he proclaimed that 'Churchill would have approved' (Robertson, 2020) of

Centre for Liberty Report on CANZUK

CANZUK, it is not unfair to argue that CANZUK, if cooperating in the ways argued by this policy paper (below), could be a dominate international power on par or beyond that of Iran or even the Russian Federation.

For that to be taken seriously CANZUK will need to balance between spreading democracy and ensuring that we do not invade places that very clearly do not want it (which damages the trust in the Anglospheric ideals domestically) is what the next part will attempt to solve. It is a careful balancing act but Collier has previously suggested a policy direction that could solve this (Collier, 2009) has suggested (outside of the CANZUK context) a route to that could be taken by the four kingdoms to tread the line between the two, especially as the forces of tyranny in China, the Russian Federation and Iran continue to grow in influence. The United States of America cannot be on its own, given the failures of democratic spread in the 21st century, to be the only democratic global power and as the clear other side of the Anglosphere, CANZUK should be in a strong position to be the change needed on the international stage.

The second area in which CANZUK could make the difference in international affairs is within global institutions, especially the United Nation. Many problems with the United Nations can be identified and it is a far cry from some of the 19th century thoughts on having an international system not all of governments but only those which are 'self-governing and sovereign nations' (Scruton, 2006, p.22) unlike the current juntas, despots and theocratic extremists infecting the United Nations General Assembly.

However, the greatest problems are contained within the Security Council, the only body of the United Nations able to sanction military action. Of the five members with veto power, two are clearly not fit for the role of creating international law and allowing military force to be used for good. The Security Council just about worked when there was goodwill following the Second World War and also worked when China was represented by what has become the government in modern Twain whilst at the same time the (then) USSR refused to participate, however briefly. At that point, it was essentially three democracies and a pushover government with veto power. Between the two changes, the loss of good will and arrival of both Russian and Communist Chinese power onto the Security Council, the United Nations has lost its effectiveness. The inability of the United Nations to cooperate on the major wars and emergencies of the day, whether it is resolving ongoing conflicts in Syria and Libya or dealing with immediate emergencies such as the 2021 coup d'état in Burma.

This should not be of surprise, given the theory of political decay. The concept was originally developed by Samuel Huntingdon (Fukuyama, 2011, p.139) but subsequently expanded upon by Fukuyama, a student of Huntingdon. The theory of political decay is based upon the premise that 'There should be no general presumption that political order, once it emerges, will be self-sustaining.' (Fukuyama, 2011, p.139) Whilst history, in some schools of thought, is seen as a general march towards progress, potentially with a set inevitable endpoint or an endpoint that has been stumbled upon (Fukuyama, 1992), 'there was no reason to assume that political development was any more likely than political decay.' (Fukuyama, 2011, p.139) Changes in the political, social or economic context of the society of the system in which an institution operates over time changes the effectiveness of institutions. All institutions, the United Nations included, 'are created to meet the demands of specific circumstances.' (Fukuyama, 2014, p.463) When those circumstances change, the ability of the institution to function as intended changes as well. It is clear, with the good will following the Second World War long gone and the obstructiveness of both China and the Russian Federation on the Security Council, that the United Nations has undergone political decay.

It is obvious that simply proposing reform will not be enough to force China and the Russian Federation to cooperate in the United Nations. As Fukuyama argued, 'elite groups have a stake in existing institutional arrangements… will defend the status quo… even when the society as a whole would benefit from an institutional change' (Fukuyama, 2011, p.454). It is clear that on humanitarian issues and the cause of freedom, China and the Russian Federation will, like all those who benefit from political decay, 'veto change because for them the change is negative.' (Fukuyama, 2011, p.454)

Therefore, conditions need to be created to combat the power that dictatorships have in the United Nations to force them to compromise. It will only be through, whilst maintaining the importance of a rules based international order, reducing the influence of the veto in the Security Council, without rendering the United Nations redundant, that positive change will be created. Ultimately, 'The ability of societies to innovate institutionally thus depends on whether they can neutralize existing political stakeholders holding vetoes over reform.' (Fukuyama, 2011, p.456) This should not be seen as separate from the balance between promoting democracy because the two issues can, and realistically can only be, dealt with in conjunction with each other (as argued below). Only through promoting democracy, without committing troops to where they are not welcome or don't have a realistic chance of succeeding, will the influence and ability of China and the Russian Federation to use the United Nations as an obstruction be reduced.

Centre for Liberty Report on CANZUK

This will be how this policy paper proceeds. Firstly, there will be a look at how the CANZUK Kingdoms could develop, on a case-by-case basis, treaties to use their military strength to promote democracy, the rule of law and protection of minorities through cooperation with existing governments. This, due to the shared belief in the value of democracy and the rule of law and the military power of the CANZUK Kingdoms combined, is best achieved at the CANZUK level. That will be developed through adapting work previously done by Collier to the CANZUK situation. The second point will be looking at how this could be used to create the conditions for change within international institutions, such as the United Nations. It will look at how CANZUK cooperation, with a look at how a shared CANZUK seat on the United Nations Security Council could activate the conditions created by suggested foreign policy. These will follow on from each other, as the conditions for change in the United Nations will require the shift in foreign policy that is argued before it.

Ciarán Reed

Foreign Policy by Consent

This part of the policy paper will attempt to demonstrate a policy position that will balance a series of competing aims to produce a coherent foreign policy that could be implemented by the governments of the CANZUK Kingdoms. There are three main competing interests: the benefit of acting at the CANZUK level against the independence of each kingdom; the need to commit military force to protect democratic governments compared to ensuring that troops are not sent inappropriately; and the want to maintain a rules-based international order whilst devaluing the role of dictatorships in the United Nations.

The first point to emphasise is the maintaining of the independence of foreign policy of each of the four kingdoms. It is reasonable to expect that none of the four governments would be willing to lose control over their foreign policy on any level. It would not only be against their own interests but against the interests of their electorates and the belief in the Westminster style of democracy, which requires each for the four parliaments to be sovereign. Therefore, any shared foreign policy must have the highest level of tailorability possible for each of the CANZUK Kingdoms, with the government being able to decide their involvement in CANZUK schemes on an individual basis. That, fairly clearly, has to be balanced with the desirability of acting on the CANZUK level. The increased military and diplomatic power of acting as a cohesive unit is an advantage that should not be ignored. Furthermore, the commonality of belief in democracy and liberty along with the linguistic and cultural closeness make cooperation realistic and the interests of the four CANZUK Kingdoms on international affairs similar.

The second competing set of interests is the desire for spreading democracy which needs to be compared with ensuring that military force is not committed where it will not be effective and also produces further considerations. It is clear that some level of military force will be needed in at least the protection of democracy, if not the spread of it. Democracy, especially in the developing world, is frail, with coup d'états (such as the one seen in Burma in 2021) not uncommon. Therefore, a policy position which could help provide military assistance for the protection of democracy would be ideal and necessary if it is to be maintained in the developing world. This needs to be balanced with ensuring that CANZUK soldiers are not committed in places where either they are not welcome or do not have a realistic chance of succeeding. What should be avoided are situations like Afghanistan or Iraq, where there is no clear government to take over and limited chance of being able to withdraw from combat. Without such a balance, either democracies would be under threat of being overturned by military force from within their own borders or the CANZUK militaries will end committed to theatres of war without the ability to withdraw and sustain heavy losses. Neither extreme is desirable and a nuanced and detailed position will be required to ensure that policy does not lead to those undesirable outcomes in any situation.

The final competing set of aims is the want for an international rules-based order and reducing the power of undesirable governments in the United Nations. All four CANZUK Kingdoms, by virtue of the belief in the rule of law that is inherent in the Anglospheric identity (as argued above), are leaders in defending international law. They promote the need for governments to be bound by their treaties and respect international conventions. This is required for democracies to function, with the rule of law being a necessity for the elections to work (as argued below) and the international laws is a part of that.

However, the United Nations, with the decay that has taken place in it (as argued above), is a crucial part of the international legal system but needs reform, rather than abolition to keep international law- and peace-making mechanisms. For reform to happen, the importance of it (for the moment) needs to be subverted (as argued above). Therefore, a balance should be struck between: the deploying military force; respecting international law; undermining the power of China and the Russian Federation in the United Nations; and keeping the United Nations relevant for once it is reformed.

This is where an over the horizon consent-based protection agreement, enforced by rapid response forces, based upon the current government of a county building the conditions necessary for a transition to democracy would provide a cost-effective platform to attempt to achieve all of the goals and balances stated.

The premise of the main viable policy within Collier's *Guns, Wars & Votes* was that the developed world is in a position to use the internal violence of the countries of what he termed 'the bottom billion' (Collier, 2009) as a way of improving the level of development in those countries. He wrote that 'The core proposal… is a strategy whereby a small intervention from the international community can harness the political violence of the bottom billion. This powerful force that to date has been so destructive can be turned into an advantage, becoming the defender of democracy rather than its antithesis.' (Collier, 2009, p.10) The policy would have the developed world provide voluntary security guarantees to countries that agree to certain international standards of governance and democracy. This would see, in exchange for achieving goals in political development (described below), the guarantor countries commit to put down any coup d'état or other violent attempt to remove the government that is transitioning or has achieved democracy. That would allow developing governments to start lifting repression without the fear of being overthrown as a result. This is necessary as 'coups are at least as likely to break out in democracies as in autocracies' (Collier, 2009, p.146) and without repressive tactics, governments are more likely to be overthrown by them, meaning security support is needed in democracies in the developing world. That means that democracies in the developing world need protecting from coups d'états if they are to be sustainable in the long term and not be overthrown by minority voices in the country at hand.

Where the concept becomes interesting is how that protection could be achieved with minimal troops. The agreement will be secured with an over the horizon rapid response force, leaving minimal troops in situ in each guaranteed country. This is based upon both the British experience in Sierra Leone, where 'For the past few years there have been only 80 British troops stationed in Sierra

Leone' (Collier, 2009, p.85) and the French experience of previous support to Francophone Africa until the 1990s. The way the force would work is through having a minimal presence in each guaranteed country which included an air base or a sea port. A much larger force would be situated at a regional base that covered a large number of countries. In the event of force being needed in the country, the troops already in the country would protect the route into it whilst the rapid response force would be specialised to be capable of moving into an area in a short period of time (ideally 24 hours). That would mean that with only a small number of forces permanent in the country, a much larger force which can cover whole regions could be deployed when needed. The agreement would be an exchange of security guarantee where developed countries would set up a base and ensure that a force could be deployed in an emergency situation, which would be used to defend against attempts to undemocratically overthrow the government in return for the developing countries meeting targets (as set out below).

Since Collier wrote *Guns, Wars & Votes* the international community hasn't taken this policy as a collective. However, for a number of very neat reasons, it can be, with a few tweaks, aptly suited to being delivered by CANZUK. The policy would work by each of the four CANZUK Kingdoms making treaties with countries in the developing world whereby the developing country agree to achieving some reforms in a certain time in return for the four CANZUK Kingdoms agreeing to intervene, militarily if needed, to overturn any non-democratic change of government. That would mean that in the event of a coup d'état, the CANZUK Kingdoms would deploy troops into the developing country to maintain the reformist and (once the goals had been achieved) democratic government. By having the military intervention based upon British involvement in Sierra Leone, the CANZUK Kingdoms would not need a large military presence in each country but instead just a small base in which troops can enter the country and a rapid response force based outside, which could cover a whole region of countries. That would keep the financial cost of the project lower than having troops in each country and mean that, outside of times of emergency, there would not be a large foreign (CANZUK) military presence in the guaranteed countries.

The CANZUK Kingdoms would also, by virtue of being committed to where they have treaties, tacitly be in agreement that they would not overturn a coup d'état in a country where the incumbent government hadn't signed up to political development and governments that agree to the protocol would be at their own liberty to leave the agreement at any point. That is where Collier's statement of how the democratic world 'can harness the political violence of the bottom billion' (Collier, 2009, p.189) comes into play. Governments in the developing world 'are more likely to lose power to their army than through any other route.' (Collier, 2009, p.8) Furthermore, 'Usually the violence is internal' (Collier, 2009, p.7). What this means is that for a government in the developing world, they are more likely to be overthrown militarily than by holding free and fair elections. In the event of seeing a dictator fall to a coup d'état, there will be a push towards agreeing to the CANZUK guarantee as it will most likely be the safest way of keeping power for governments in the developing world.

That is exaggerated in situations where a country withdraws from the CANZUK agreement. Given that it is most likely that it would happen in the aftermath of an election lost by the incumbent, there would already be a government in waiting if the army so wished to put it into power and agree to the protocol. Where it becomes even more ingenious is that in that situation where the army overthrows a government that recently left the agreement but chooses to keep power for itself, the threat of a further coup d'état is significantly higher, due to research that demonstrates that coups make future coups more likely (Collier, 2009, p.206-207). That is because, once proving a coup can work, the next rank down of officers can essentially do the same thing as their superiors did to take power. The only way, once a coup d'état has been done in that situation following an election, to protect against further coups is with the help of outside intervention, such as joining the protocol. It gives an incentive to the military in those countries to, in the event they have taken power, transition to democracy as military governments installed by coups are inherently unstable. Military governments, following coups, have proven themselves in the past to be able to transition to democracy (Collier, 2009, p.206-207), making this not unrealistic as a prospect.

This leaves the situation where governments are able to freely choose to make security arrangements with the CANZUK Kingdoms that set goals for transitioning to a proper democracy. In the event of political violence in those states, CANZUK would intervene to protect the government moving in the correct direction. If the guaranteed government chooses to leave of its own volition, or is expelled from the agreement for not keeping to its terms, it is left to its own devices and any future government, however it obtained recognised power would be welcome to re-join. The same goes for countries that chose not to agree to such an arrangement, in the event of political violence, the government would be left by the CANZUK Kingdoms to its own devices.

There are a number of crucial areas to highlight, namely how it fits into the foreign policy objectives that CANZUK should be striving towards (argued above). Implementing this policy, with the four CANZUK

Centre for Liberty Report on CANZUK

Kingdoms as the guarantors (rather than the whole international community who very clearly haven't taken this idea forward), would manage to solve the issues of: keeping a rules-based order whilst limiting the power of dictatorships in the United Nations; being able to use military force to spread democracy without committing troops to futile and costly (in both lives and money) wars; and having a CANZUK policy that does not infringe on the sovereignty of each kingdom.

The first point to develop is how it can keep a rules-based order whilst not needing the United Nations to agree to sanction military deployment. Ultimately, the agreement would simply be a treaty between sovereign governments. It would be four kingdoms agreeing to enter a partnership with a legal and internationally recognised government, a bit like how countries already agree to help with military training or set up bases in other countries. It is outside of the remit of the United Nations Security Council. In the event of a coup d'état, whilst the United Nations Security Council may choose to issue a resolution on the matter, the intervention by the CANZUK Kingdoms would simply be the upholding of an agreement, not an invasion or unsanctioned intervention in a foreign country. What this would mean is that the CANZUK Kingdoms would have areas in which they could deploy force for the security of democracy when needed without going through the

United Nations whilst still being within the bounds of freely made treaties and the rules based international order, just as the United Kingdom didn't need United Nations approval to intervene in Sierra Leone because it was brought in by the pe-existing internationally recognised government (Greenstock, 2016, p.247). The more countries that agree to such an arrangement, the more countries would be safe from regression into tyranny being held by blockages in the United Nations. In events where CANZUK needed to provide military assistance, basing intervention in treaty would ensure that the accusation of interfering in the internal matters of a foreign country was unfounded because it had permission from the legally recognised government to do so. It would therefore limit the ability of dictatorships, especially China and the Russian Federation, to attempt to declare the promotion of democracy with military force (when done through this policy) illegitimate and limit their power to stop it in the United Nations without destroying the remit of the United Nations in countries outside of the treaties, thereby maintaining some power in the United Nations despite limiting the power of China and the Russia Federation and supporting a rules based international order.

The second point to develop is how, by using treaty and agreement, can ensure that troops are only deployed where they are wanted and have a great chance of success in spreading sustainable democracy. This needs to be developed in two directions, the military aspect and the creation of a truly democratic system.

The democratic side is what the actual goal of intervention is and therefore will be dealt with first. A point that Collier spent a significant time dwelling on was how, where democracy is only done in name, 'creating the façade is likely to frustrate democratic accountability rather than fast track it.' (Collier, 2009, p.8) Whilst elections are clearly a part of democracy, without efforts to limit corruption and violence, democracy does not exist. Scruton noted, following his experience with resistance movements in Eastern Europe, 'how unimportant a part of democracy are elections, in comparison with the enduring institutions and public spirit that make elected politicians accountable.' (Scruton, 2014, p.14) There are two things needed for democracy to truly be viable, those being the creation of a modern state and a collective identity.

Elections are evolutionary affairs, where politicians compete for career survival with limited positive outcomes for them (a limited number of elected positions), somewhat like how animals compete for limited resources of food. Those who have the right skills are re-elected, those who come with something new that is good are elected for the first time and those who are incumbent but failed to win enough votes are forced out, like an extinct species that failed to adapt. In a functioning democratic system, there needs to be rules to ensure that elections are free and fair. Without rules and without the ability to enforce them, elections can turn bad. Instead of that evolutionary pressure on politicians being for creating good policy, the pressure selects those who can bribe, threaten and corrupt the count the best. Instead of being who can set a vision for improving a country, only those who can win a contest for who can manipulate the ballot box the most effectively, regardless of the damage it does to the country, continue to have a career in politics. This not only removes the benefit of democracy, accountability to the people where the government acts in the interest of the citizens, but also removes any chance of that being achieved. Ultimately, 'If being honest and competent does not give you an election advantage, then the honest and competent will be discouraged.' (Collier, 2009, p.27) What that will leave is only the corrupt and the bad to the point at which 'If honest people are unlikely to win and so do not come forward as candidates, then voters lack even the choice of a decent leader.' (Collier, 2009, p.28) This cycle is why implementing elections before institutions are developed will create the situation where for those elections 'The more effective strategies are also incompatible with the rule of law' (Collier, 2009, p.46), which creates a 'Darwinian struggle for political survival in which the winner is the one who adopts the most cost-effective means of attracting votes. In absence of restraints the most cost-effective means are simply not going to be good governance: that option is surely way down the list.' (Collier, 2009 p.40) Not only does that limit the ability of democracy to improve but, as pointed out, will limit good governance. It is therefore in the interest of not just spreading democracy but also creating better governance in the developing world, which is clearly needed, to build a viable state before forcing elections onto a country.

This is where Fukuyama becomes instructive again. He argued that there are three components to having a modern state which need to be active to, as he put it, achieve 'getting to Denmark' (Fukuyama, 2014, pp.24-27). Those components are state-building, the rule of law and accountability in government (Fukuyama, 2011). Each of them is contingent on the previous one, with the rule of law requiring institutions, such as courts and tax raising, to be functional before it can be implemented and accountability requires rules to be above the ruler, therefore needing the rule of law before accountability. If democracy is to be implemented in the developing world, both state-building and the rule of law need to be implemented first. Collier was well aware of the need for institutions to come first (even though he was writing just before Fukuyama), noting that 'We did not do it in a single leap: dictatorship to liberal democracy. We have been unrealistic in expecting that these societies could in one step make a transition that has historically been made in several distinct steps.' (Collier, 2009, p.49) In some cases, including the Anglosphere, even 'accountability was in place well in advance of competitive elections.' (Collier, 2009, p.186) We had parliament as a stable body capable of challenging and when needed removing the government (and in some cases even the monarch) before we had democratic elections. We also had a strong rule of law through common law to facilitate that (Hannan, 2013). Whilst trying to create accountability without elections appears to have only been possible through organic development, it is noteworthy for emphasising how rushing to elections in developing countries is not the right strategy if we are to aid the implementation of democracy.

Therefore, it seems that other factors should be emphasised, before elections, in the creation of terms for security arrangements. A focus should be made on ensuring that the government has secure infrastructure, with the ability to supply citizens with public goods, that are free from corruption. For countries starting right from the beginning, with limited to no government beforehand (such as if a newly independent state or a country that had been severely damaged by civil war), that should be priority in the first set of terms for the arrangements for security. There should be a time scale laid for completion of such tasks and offers of aid to support should be given but not made a condition of the treaty, as the hope is to achieve the end goal of the country being a self-sustaining democracy. If, without reasonable reasons why, the government does not achieve the goals, they will have been seen as not fulfilling their side of the contract and it will, as a result, no longer be valid, leaving the government to fend for itself with the implications thereof (as described above). The second aim should be to achieve the rule of law. Again, (as argued above) this is needed before democracy can be achieved (Fukuyama, 2011). An emphasis on the independence of the judiciary should be made, with the same conditions as the previous part, with countries that agree to it being protected by over the horizon rapid response units of CANZUK soldiers who would act in the event of a coup d'état, with the expectation that the treaty would lapse if the guaranteed country does not create such institutions within an allotted time frame. Only then should there be a move to making the treaty focus on free and fair elections, as the other two are preconditions of real democracy. There should, once those conditions have been met, be an agreed set of standards for elections, with observers from the four kingdoms allowed to ensure that they are being met. Again, in the circumstances that those conditions aren't met, the contract should be seen as void. However, given the risks of doing so (as described above) it is unlikely that a government would do that, and even if they did, the military would have a high incentive to reverse the decision, with the risk of more junior officers doing the same thing if the upper staff don't act adding to the encouragement for actions. Those would create the conditions for an effective democracy before then implementing elections, which should make them more sustainable. That may require an evolving constitution, where the guaranteed country has a constitution has an inbuilt change instead of having the usual static constitution with amendment procedures but how it the constitutions should be fashioned for each country should (as argued above) be decided internally and not by CANZUK.

The second branch is a shared identity. Democracy and identity are linked, with a shared identity being the main way in which a democracy can encourage the losers of elections to accept the result other than through repressive violence. There are many benefits to having a shared national identity (as argued above) but that requirement of it in democracy needs to be emphasised. At the most fundamental level, there is the question of why people are one country, expressed by Hannan as 'without a demos, there is not democracy.' (Hannan, 2013) Without an explanation of who the people in a country are and how they are one shared identity it is implausible to believe they can they be encouraged people to vote in the interests of their community, especially if they do not feel they are a part of a broader community of the nation.

However, the problem runs deeper than that. The question Scruton posed was why do 'We accept to be ruled by laws and decisions made by politicians with whom we disagree' (Scruton, 2017, p.7)? Most of the time, the citizens do disagree with their elected politicians. Over 56% of British voters who showed up to the 2019 general election didn't vote for the Conservative and Union Party but they are still the governing party. Over 75% of French voters who turned out to the polls did not vote for Emmanuel Macron as their first choice in the last French Presidential elections. That is even before the question of whether the individual voter's first choice is on the ballot paper, with over 55% of those who showed up to the Republic primaries in 2016, almost 52% of those who voted not voting for Barack Obama in the 2008 Democrat primaries and no chose via open primaries in most democratic states. At best, democracies tend to give the election to the candidate who has made it onto the ballot paper who has the largest plurality of the vote but even then, even in the CANZUK Kingdoms, that hasn't always happened, with the 1952 United Kingdom general election and 1979 Canadian federal election. For various reasons, including Arrow's Impossibility Theorem and people generally just not agreeing on politics, democracy cannot give everyone the outcome they want. Therefore, there needs to be a reason why people don't 'refuse to be governed by those they never voted for' (Scruton, 2017, p.7).

The 'pre-political loyalty' (Scruton, 2017, p,7) of national identity is required, as it forces the government to act in the interests of all in the country, not just its voters. Countries without a shared sense of identity cannot function due to the competition for shared resources between identity groups. Countries that have built a shared identity tend to be better governed as a result (Miguel, 2004). The problem is when identity voting below the national level takes place. In an electoral competition in which ethnic competition takes place is troubling on a number of levels. When electoral competition is about ethnicity, the ability to judge candidates by their actions is lessened. Furthermore, electoral competition can go in two directions. It can either go the way of Papua New Guinea and the Solomon Islands where ethnic and tribal loyalties lead to local leaders being elected to parliament to 'use his or her influence to direct government resources back to the wantok' (Fukuyama, 2011, p.xiv) in a manner that makes, to 'many foreigners, the behaviour of Melanesian politicians looks like political corruption' (Fukuyama, 2011, p.xiv). Without the belief in a broader national identity, there is no incentive to improve the whole country but instead to drag resources to one's own identity group. The second route is that of extremism through coalition negotiations. Collier noted Northern Ireland as an example of this (Collier, 2009, p.57). Since the Good Friday Agreement, there has been a shift from moderate to more extreme parties. This, Collier argued, as due to the coalition system in Northern Ireland (Collier, 2009, p.57). Voters are encouraged to vote for more extreme parties when they know there will be a coalition across identity lines as it gives them the best point from which to start negotiations and work inwards. A moderate Unionist trying to find common ground to build a coalition with a Nationalist extremist would end up with an agreement skewed to the Nationalist side. That is one of the factors behind why there has been a shift for Unionists from the UUP to the DUP and for Nationalists from the SDLP to Sinn Féin, both of those being a shift from a moderate party to a more extreme one. This is being seen in 2021 as well, with a genuine threat that the DUP may be hit by the even more extreme TUV over the DUP's willingness to have previously compromised with the Conservative Party in the House of Commons and not being harsh enough on the Northern Ireland Protocol (Forsyth, 2021, p.10). In the case of Northern Ireland, the Good Friday Agreement has done a very good job of keeping the peace but if it had not been for cooperation between the governments of the

Republic of Ireland and the United Kingdom, it is questionable whether the territory would have been governed for large periods of time in the past two decades due to how often coalitions cannot be made. If that model was transferred to a place without two central governments to step in, it might literally be an anarchy as the government couldn't function. Therefore, going to the extremes in politics is advantageous when there are negotiations across identity groups. Neither outcomes, that of elections becoming a game of raiding the communal resources for one's own identity group or extremism in coalition is desirable.

As a result, if the aim of the CANZUK foreign policy should be to promote democracy in the long term, rather than the short term, it must be a part of the arrangement that the guaranteed governments must work towards a shared identity. This could be done through the creation of national symbols or promotion of a shared language but it is absolutely necessary if democracy is to function and therefore must be included in the demands of the treaties alongside the building of state institutions, the rule of law and free and fair elections. National identity does not need to replace ethnic, religious or political identities. A good example of how this can be achieved was the Netherlands and Flanders, which for many years operated a pillarised society, in which the four groups (Catholics, Protestants, liberals and socialists) each ran their own societies within the nation as a whole (Rountree, 1910). This allowed for the different identities to continue to function within the country, keeping separate. However, even in that situation, it still required an overarching identity (Wintle, 2000) with a clear sense of what it meant to be Dutch (Spiecker and Steutel, 2001) for the separate identity to be able to cooperate, especially with how separate they were, with different schools, shops and social clubs (Rountree, 1910) existing. Whilst this model has gone out of favour (Hellemans, 2020) and is in decline (Vanderstraeten, 2002), it demonstrates that national identity doesn't need to eliminate ethnic, religious or political ones, they still need to be in existence for democracy to work and therefore, creating a sense of national identity should be one of the conditions within the treaties created by the CANZUK Kingdoms.

What the policy of consent-based over the horizon security treaties therefore does is allow for an achievable pathway to democracy to be set forwards, with it being based upon consent of the sovereign government and the people it will be accountable to in elections, the citizens. There are two more quick points of note to add to the democratic side before moving to the military advantages of this policy. The first is that what style of democracy is implemented should not be prescribed. Whilst, obviously, there is a clear tendency towards Westminster parliamentary systems between the four CANZUK

Kingdoms, this should not be forced upon a country. As long as it has the institutions of government functional, the rule of law and a form of elections that are free and fair, the guaranteed country should be allowed to choose its own path. If a guaranteed country wants a different separation of power, such as a presidential system, they should be more than welcome to create that constitution. If a guaranteed country wants to use an electoral system different to those that are found in the CANZUK Kingdoms (which are already diverse), such as a two-round runoff, they should be free to do so. The intention of this policy is not to tell the developing world how it should act or govern itself but instead provide the security needed for those in power who wish to transition to democracy to be successful. It should not be the intention of the policy to have the CANZUK governments decide the politics of the countries at hand or their constitutional arrangements, beyond those needed to make a mature democracy. The second point is that also, the citizens of a country should be allowed to decide to leave the arrangements. If the guaranteed country elects a government that does not want CANZUK troops guaranteeing its democratic security, that country should be left alone. The whole point is to base the spread of democracy in consent and therefore, if the citizens withdraw their consent to the treaty, their wishes should be respected.

Centre for Liberty Report on CANZUK

The military advantages are a multi-layered affair. The two main areas they impact are ensuring that troops are only deployed to where they have a realistic chance of success and where the danger is limited. The first point comes from the treaties being made with already existing governments. The previous paragraphs looked at the process to transitioning to democracy, however a number of the countries that could agree to such arrangements are likely to be further down the path than not having reached step one. These will be already existing governments with their own arrangements for collecting tax and providing public goods. There will most probably already be some form of police force, courts and civil service, even if those organs of the state are corrupt. By working with pre-existing governments, the process will be that of reform rather than creation. This will avoid the problems faced in Iraq of not having the basic infrastructure to implement policies and having to make up political leadership (with the constitution needed for that) after troops are on the ground (Greenstock, 2016). Making agreements with governments means that the CANZUK militaries will not need to act as local law enforcement or rebuild the state from the ground up. This means that power vacuums, the likes of which were seen in Afghanistan and Iraq, will not develop, limiting the formation of militias, meaning that they are less likely to kill CANZUK soldiers in a bid for power. This, combined, means that democracy is more likely to become a reality as there are already power structures to work with and, by virtue of them agreeing to the treaty, are likely to be cooperative.

The second point is that the military is also unlikely to face the same level of resistance, even beyond having the consent of the people because of it being a democratic system (which should decrease the chance of a truly popular revolt). By being an over the horizon agreement, large numbers of troops do not need to be stationed in each guaranteed country, giving little opportunity for scandal or resentment. However, the threat of that rapid response force will scare people into not forming rebel groups. Rebel groups, when faced with an elected government, are unlikely to be able to overthrow the physical force of said government, the country's citizens and the CANZUK Kingdoms in one go. As a result, the chance of success being low means that groups won't try. Knowing that CANZUK will intervene means local soldiers are unlikely to mutiny over personal issues such as a lack of pay, decreasing the threat of violence from smaller disputes as well. That means that by providing the guarantee, the chance of having to intervene is actually lowered. That is backed up by the data as well. 'Statistically, the [previous French] guarantee significantly and substantially reduced the risk of conflict by nearly three-quarters.' (Collier, 2009, p.86) Furthermore, only the overly illogical will even attempt to give overthrowing the government a go knowing that CANZUK will arrive and therefore, any attempts at rebellions will most probably be disorganised and low in moral, making victory for democratic forces easier. That does require the commitment to be taken seriously and for those in guaranteed countries to believe CANZUK will actually intervene as promised. However, given the seriousness of the policy and what a CANZUK Prime Minister would look like to their respective parliament and electorate if they rescinded on the agreements, the promise of military intervention in the agreed circumstances should be ensured (Collier, 2009, pp.209-210). Taken seriously, almost nobody would dare go against what the citizens, guaranteed government and large CANZUK military power would want. As a result, between the small presence needed at most of the time and lowered chance of rebellion as a result of agreements (Collider, 2009, p.86), most citizens of guaranteed countries will never see a CANZUK solider. From their perspective, the effect of CANZUK soldiers will be felt in security but their daily lives will not be tampered with.

Therefore, on the military front, this policy will not only ensure that troops are only deployed to where there is a viable government capable of convincing the CANZUK Kingdoms to support them and has the capacity of already being the government with the ability to engage in international treaty making but also ensure that when troops needed to go into combat, it will be in favourable circumstances. As a result, this policy solves the problem of being able to use military force to spread democracy and not committing troops to unwinnable places. By having clear criteria – on the matter of overthrowing a government – on when to intervene or not, the publics of the CANZUK Kingdoms know what their troops will be committed to. That also means that, due to having agreed on what situations troops can act without the need for United Nations approval, the embarrassing situations of democratic forces watching mass violence and even genocides should not happen. Furthermore, within agreements, research can be used to ensure extra troops are deployed at times when violence is more likely, such as in post conflict situations where 'In the year before the election the risk of going back to violence is very sharply reduced: the society looks to have reverted back to safety. But in the year after the election the risk explodes upwards.' (Collier, 2009, p.81) Having more troops on the ground to defend the basis where the rapid response force would land at the time of an election and in the following year compared to the year before an election would further help ensure security in guaranteed countries and could make, with fewer troops in the year before an election, the cost savings of having troops cover a whole region even greater. Altogether, the use of the

Centre for Liberty Report on CANZUK

CANZUK militaries as a deterrent to those overthrowing governments that are cooperating in creating the conditions for and transitioning to real democracy should ensure that force is only applied where it has a chance (through existing institutions) of succeeding in a cost-efficient system that would promote democracy and stability.

The third of the three policy balances for CANZUK that the over the horizon security guarantees provide is the ability to keep each kingdom sovereign. Each guaranteed country should be dealt with on a case-by-case basis. The differences in circumstances across each country means that different goals would need to be set for their governments to move them further down the path of having a mature democracy. Therefore, despite the military arrangements being similar across each country, the details of what needs to be achieved by each government will vary, meaning that each country will require a separate treaty. It would be desirable that each country was guaranteed by all four CANZUK Kingdoms. Doing so would provide extra legitimacy, rather than it seeming like one kingdom pushing its military onto a developing country, and create a pressure to act when needed, with the diplomatic pressure of the three other kingdoms who are also party forcing action when coup d'états are attempted, thereby making the guarantee more credible, something that is necessary to limit the threat of them happening in the first place (see above). However, each of the four kingdoms will be welcome to sign or not sign treaties as they please. Each should be acting as a separate signature. Therefore, if one or more of the kingdoms have a particular aversion, for whatever reason, to guaranteeing a country, they do not have to be party to that individual treaty. Doing treaties on a country-by-country basis will ensure that each government can chose which countries it helps and the parliaments of the four kingdoms can, within the constitutional mechanisms provided by each kingdom, advise or veto their own kingdoms involvement in a particular country without changing the involvement of the other kingdoms. As pointed out earlier in the paragraph, doing it at the CANZUK level has its advantages for diplomatic and political reasons and also could help with military intelligence and the efficient spread of forces, and therefore should be encouraged. By not making that mandatory, each kingdom's independence and sovereignty is protected, just like with signing separate trade deals with other countries, whilst still having the benefits of CANZUK cooperation in most cases.

Within that CANZUK frame, it would probably not be all four kingdoms actively engaging with each of the guaranteed countries at one time. The regional level at which the rapid response units would operate at will make it more efficient to assign each of the for kingdom's different geographic areas of coverage. Rapid response units are effective and cost efficient because they can cover whole regions rather than just one individual country and therefore, having each kingdom provide the forces for different regions helps protect those advantages. That does not undermine the collective nature of the action, with it still being an advantage to have the diplomatic advice and support to give the one kingdom covering a particular region to act if the other three are party to all the agreements. Furthermore, it would give flexibility for the kingdoms to change which countries they directly cover without needing to change the terms of the treaties and adds to the threat to potential anti-democratic forces within a guaranteed country to have the other three kingdoms being in the legal position, by treaty, to intervene, even if they are not the primary military force expected to act if needed. How the regions should be divided up would be down to which countries agree to treaties and should consider the interests of each kingdom in the region at hand and the ability of each kingdom to deploy military force in each place. It wouldn't be surprising to see Australia take the lead in south east Asia given the proximity and the United Kingdom to take the lead in Sierra Leone and any Mediterranean countries, given the United Kingdom already has an existing military presence in Sierra Leone and parts of the Mediterranean, including Gibraltar and Cyprus, from which it can launch military missions. However, without knowing the minutiae of which countries would agree, giving definitive answers is not possible at this time.

It would also most probably be advisable that whichever kingdom would take the lead in military protection in a particular country should take the lead on other matters with that country. That is not to say that the other three kingdoms should not be present but that whichever kingdom would be the primary military actor should, in diplomatic terms, hold the pen. This would help ensure that military and political policies were lined up in each country, with the same kingdom being the lead on both, and (by giving each kingdom different regions) stop any one of the four kingdoms from taking over the whole global policy.

Initially, not many governments may agree. It could be the case that only one, Sierra Leone, agrees and only because it essentially has that arrangement already. However, the number should be expected to grow. As CANZUK proves that the intention to commit forces within the boundaries of the arrangements becomes clearer and pressure of coup d'états grow within pretend democracies and dictatorships (as described above) it should be expected to see more countries join, especially after events of post-election violence (Collier, 2009, p.81) in neighbouring countries for security. Furthermore, if there was a coup d'état put down by CANZUK through this system, it should be expected that more countries would join as well given it would prove both the credibility of the threat and the policy.

The true test of the policy and the success criteria that it should be judged by must be long term. The aim is to create stable governments that are functioning modern states, with the three pillars needed for that: state-building; the rule of law; and accountability. Democracies, when created properly, are the best way of fulfilling all three conditions. That is not something that will happen instantly, with the advent of liberal democracy with a universal franchise still somewhat new, having only come about in the last 100 to 200 years (dependent on the kingdom) in the Anglospheric civilisation that has existed for well over 1,500 years. Therefore, the end goal of declaring success should not be a short-term aim, even though stopping coup d'états today and having countries achieve success points along the way should be celebrated. One somewhat ambitious success criterion which would test the system would be to declare the policy a true success when a country has become so stable, its government so trustworthy and its reputation so strong that it transfers from being a guaranteed country to a guarantor for others. At that point, it would be recognised by both the four CANZUK

Kingdoms and the country that it agrees to join the treaty with as a democracy both trustworthy and capable of providing such a defence. It will probably take decades to get to such a stage and it would not have to be a Westminster style democracy to achieve such as goal (as any democratic military power that all other parties to the treaty trust can sign) but it would be a sure sign that a country had developed to be politically stable, democratically accountable and economically strong enough to have an excess military that it could use for benign use. It would demonstrate that CANZUK had helped the country make such a success of itself that it had become an equal partner not just in its own territory, as it should always be, but an equal partner on the international stage.

The over the horizon security guarantees, in exchange for the reforms set out above, would help provide answers to all of the main foreign policy questions for CANZUK, being the promotion of democracy without using inappropriate military force, the maintaining of the international rule of law whilst undermining the power of dictatorships in the United Nations and the creation of a foreign policy for CANZUK whilst still protecting the sovereignty and independence of foreign policy for each of the four kingdoms. This policy has demonstrated how CANZUK could, through cooperation, carefully help the promotion of democracy now the democratic spread following the end of the Cold War is over and the more direct approach has been proven not to work.

This should not be the only policy, even in military terms. Of course, all four kingdoms should still engage in other appropriate action but only that, appropriate action. Planning for every eventuality is impossible due to unknown unknowns but good example of appropriate action would be repelling international invasion, such as the First Gulf War to push the Iraqis out of Kuwait (and only that, not regime change), or stopping genocide. Those actions should, however, be kept to a minimum and not be the norm. This also should not be the full extent to which CANZUK cooperation should happen on international matters outside of bodies. There should always be consideration for cooperation when it comes to matters such as stopping human trafficking and non-military points, such as the cooperation that has already taken place between CANZUK on Hong Kong at the parliamentary level (United Kingdom Parliament, 2020) and governmental level along with the United States of America (Foreign ministers of Australia, Canada, New Zealand, and the United Kingdom, and the United States Secretary of State, 2020). What the policy of over the horizon security guarantees is there to do is to show one of the directions that should be headed to by CANZUK. By virtue of the global military presence of the four kingdoms are one of incredibly few powers capable of deploying substantial military force on every continent. The policy is there to provide a framework for how that can be used to create a better, more democratic and prosperous world for those in developing countries and should be seen as the main joint policy for the four kingdoms, at least at the start of CANZUK.

The rest of the substantive of this policy paper will focus on what could be done, based upon the over the horizon security guarantees being implemented across all four kingdoms as a part of their core foreign policy. The focus on international institutions and, most dramatically, cooperation on nuclear weapons is reliant upon having a clear and united front on a number of issues, with this being the clearest way that could be achieved through it creating shared military, diplomatic and development responsibilities bound by treaty.

CANZUK at the United Nations

The international governance system is very clearly in need of reform. International institutions, such as the United Nations, have stopped being functional, with many of the pressing issues of global importance being unresolved due to the distribution of power to dictatorships in the United Nations. This section will outline what a CANZUK role in a reformed international governance order would look like, following on from the assumption of the shared foreign policy (argued above). It will look at how the four CANZUK Kingdoms could use their shared roles to further the common goals of the Anglosphere.

The model for participation proposed will be based on what the Soviet Union claimed to be its model that they were operating in the United Nations, even if reality at the time it was just a poly to increase their power in the

United Nations General Assembly. This will be an attempt to balance two competing policy objectives, those being the desire to ensure that common interests of the four CANZUK Kingdoms are advanced in the most effective manner whilst, where possible, protecting the independence of each kingdom in its actions and decreasing the power of tyrannies – most notably the Russian Federation and China – on the United Nation Security Council and keeping a rules-based international order.

It is clear that all four CANZUK Kingdoms wish to be on the United Nations security Council. The United Kingdom is already one of five permanent members and as a result has a veto. The United Kingdom has this role for historic reasons. The three New Kingdoms have also shown, through their actions, that they also have ambitions on the United Nations Security Council. Australia was an elected member from 2013-2014; New Zealand an elected member from 2015-2016; and Canada stood unsuccessfully in both 2010 and 2020. The three new kingdoms would not be doing that if they did not have ambitions, goals and objectives on the United Nations Security Council. Furthermore, the severity of the criticism of the failed Canadian bids (Bolongaro, 2020) demonstrates that there is serious desire and ambition within Canada, alongside the three CANZUK Kingdoms that have successfully been on the organ in the last decade, for influence on the United Nations Security Council.

The British position on the United Nations Security Council could be used for the benefit of the other three kingdoms. This permanent veto seat, by virtue of being controlled by the British government, is therefore already under the control of a CANZUK government. This gives leverage to the United Kingdom to influence the future direction of the United Nations beyond that of most member states of the entire body of the United Nations. This should be used to initiate reform within the United Nations for the benefit of all four CANZUK Kingdoms.

Within the context of CANZUK implementing the over the horizon security treaties, the power of the United Nations in some conflicts will have been diminished. That's because (as argued above) the United Nations will not need to sanction CANZUK military intervention in the event of those conflicts. By limiting the power of the United Nations, whilst keeping it still relevant, there will be ample scope for reform. The conditions set out by Fukuyama for reform, those being 'The ability of societies to innovate institutionally thus depends on whether they can neutralize existing political stakeholders holding vetoes over reform' (Fukuyama, 2011, p.456), will have been met, as to some extent, the ability of China and the Russian Federation to stop the Anglosphere from legally intervening in favourable circumstances will have been diminished, at least for CANZUK. If China and Russian Federation want their United Nations Security Council seats to remain relevant, they will need to accept reform. How reform should be proposed will be broken into two parts. Firstly, there will be a look at the membership of the United Nations Security Council, the part which most concerns CANZUK. This will focus on what CANZUK, acting as a cohesive unit, could look like within the United Nations as a whole and how a shift in United Nations membership be implemented for each kingdom, with a potential for an increase in the power of the whole CANZUK collective. The second part will look at what types of reform could be achieved in the United Nations. This is the more flexible part of the policy towards the United Nations. All previous policies in this paper have been very focused upon what CANZUK could achieve as a collective. The emphasis on what level of reform CANZUK could help achieve United Nations and what the objectives should be with reform will be more speculative than the previous parts of this paper. What other member states would agree to and what level of negotiation would be required to achieve such reforms is unknowable. The intention of that part is to demonstrate what level of ambition should be taken with regards to reform rather than setting a definitive form of what measures must be achieved.

Centre for Liberty Report on CANZUK

The position of the United Kingdom is most certainly advantageous, with it already having access to the veto and permanent membership. It would not be surprising, therefore, if the United Kingdom's government would require any shift of power from itself to the three new kingdoms to be in exchange for wider reform. Furthermore, it is unlikely, even if conditions change (as argued above) that the United Nations would be able to be reformed without the nations initiating such a change consenting to a change in their own power as well. A shift from the United Kingdom to CANZUK (as a desirable alternative to sole UK power) would most probably be a requirement of any reform. Therefore, whilst CANZUK representation and general United Nations reform are written about separately, they are linked due to being potentially dependent upon each other.

This will start with the case for CANZUK representation on the United Nations Security Council as the most important part of the United Nations and will cover the most achievable proposal. This is not a completely novel idea, with an Anglosphere seat having been previously proposed by the member of the British House of Commons Ben Seely (Skinner, 2018, B) prior to this paper, even though it wasn't a call for a full CANZUK seat. The first point that needs to be addressed is the question of what countries should be on the Security Council. The current numerical balance between the elected member states and the permanent five in composition appears to be about correct, even if the power is skewed. The elections system for the 15 non-permanent members works and keeping the body to 20 member states appears to be enough to ensure that there is a spread of ideas whilst being small enough to be able to produce resolutions, even if they are vetoed at the moment, in a quick manner. To change the total number of countries, as a result, on the Security Council would be to medal with one of the few aspects of it that actually works today. The question is which United Nations Member States should make that composition.

There is a legitimate debate to be had around whether there should be reform of the election areas, with it being questionable whether the Eastern European zone of represent really needs to be separate representation from the rest of Europe, with its seat potentially being elected in second years as a sole seat for a combined European and Other area or being abolished all together. However, the general principle of having 15 member states on the United Nations Security Council works and the exact organisation of the non-permanent groupings but reform should be considered alongside other main proposals of this policy paper with regards to the United Nations (with suggestions below).

The permanent representation is the more important part for CANZUK. Beyond the historical aspect, there should be justification for the membership of the United Nations Security Council. The main thrust of this should be threefold: the ability of the member state to deploy conventional military force globally; the ability of the member state to deploy non-military force globally; and the ability of the member state to create mass destruction using legally owned weapons. All three of these will be discussed together as their justifications are interlinked.

Two of the four main purposes of the United Nations are to 'To keep peace throughout the world' and 'To be a centre for harmonizing the actions of nations to achieve these goals' (United Nations, 2015). The United Nations Security Council should be at the centre of this as the only body legally entitled to authorise military action, which is needed to achieve both the aim of peace and unity in that action. The permanent members should be the governments which are in the best position to achieve such goals. That is where the three criteria become important, as each criterion assesses both whether the state is capable of achieving such goals and harming them globally. A country that meets all three criteria would have the ability to deploy peacekeepers globally, engage in war with every country on Earth and launch civilisation ending weapons of mass destruction. As a result, every conflict on the planet is related to them, as at any point, by meeting those criteria, they could intervene in both military and non-military action. Having those players engaged and supporting the work of the United Nations Security Council will mean that it can physically achieve the goals set. Whilst it may be more democratic to have it so every country voted onto the Security Council, it would not involve the key stakeholders capable of solving the situation. Without every country capable of deploying force in all theatres of conflict present and being given prominence, the United Nations would not be capable of achieving the force needed behind its resolutions and those capable of physically blocking resolutions through military force would not be present and prominent in the decision-making process, giving greater incentive to ignore the United Nations and use physical force to overturn legal ruling. Furthermore, having them involved limits the spread of conflict. Countries capable of deploying force globally can spread regional conflicts into intercontinental great wars. What may appear to be localised disputes can, with powers capable of global warfare, spread quickly. This was what happened to start both world wars, which were initially a dispute in the Balkans and a dispute over German borders, which spread to create mass warfare in Africa, Asia, Western Europe and attempted conflicts in the Americas. This happened because great powers were capable of opening theatres of war across the globe and therefore, took advantage of such power to help their cause within the region that the conflict originated. If the

United Nations is to 'keep peace' it must ensure that conflicts that are regional, potentially even just civil wars, do not become great wars. By having all countries capable of deploying force globally involved in the decision making in each conflict situation at the United Nations, this chance is decreased through the agreement between those who could escalate situations out of reasonable proportion. Ultimately, the United Nations is not there to be a democratic body, it is there to 'keep pace' and be a body for 'harmonizing the actions' (United Nations, 2015) of those capable of aiding with the first aim, which force there to be permanent members with significant say of those capable of deploying all three of military force anywhere in the world; non-military force anywhere in the world; and mass destruction anywhere in the world.

It is for those reasons why, with a small amount of tweaking (described below), the current composition of the United Nations Security Council permanent members is roughly right. The G4: Brazil, Germany, India and Japan, may make a lot of noise about joining the United Nations Security Council and are assets when they are elected to the body. However, they are not needed to solve most situations. It is questionable how much military force each country is capable of deploying. The current P5 have proven that they can wage war on any continent, with the United Kingdom having engaged in South America in the Falklands War, most members have activity in the Middle East and Africa, with bases also present in Asia for all of the P5. It is questionable whether any other nation, including the G4, could achieve that. Japan, with a constitutional commitment to pacifism still there despite some level of attempted reversion (BBC News, 2015). It is therefore incapable of achieving the level of widespread deployment of force necessary. It is further questionable whether any of the other three are capable of deploying their militaries with such a global reach as needed to mean that they are permanent military threats in all situations. It is likely that Germany and India would struggle to engage in wars in South America. By the same thinking it is questionable whether Brazil could deploy effective force in all of Africa, Europe and Asia. They are most certainly key players but if the United Nations Security Council is to be a reflection of reality, a place where the key stakeholders capable of physically creating decisions are at the top table calling the shots with the aid of elected representatives of the broader international community rather than just a place that states what it wants without force (as the League of Nations was), the G4 are not appropriate for permanent membership of the Security Council. They are likely to be elected fairly regularly, with all four being known to have somewhat decent governance for large periods of time and being crucial regional and continental actors, but are not physically capable of doing what permanent membership should be achieving.

It is worth just spending a tiny bit more time on India to cover ground on weapons of mass destruction, mostly nuclear weapons. India has nuclear weapons but is outside the Treaty on Nuclear Proliferation (NTI, 2019) and, owing to not having produced a nuclear weapon before 1967, is in contravention of its content (United Nations, 1967). It is therefore not a legal nuclear power. To give India, which most probably doesn't meet the other military criteria set out, a permanent seat on the United Nations Security Council based upon it having nuclear weapons in contravention of international treaties would be to set a bad precedent for what is meant to be an international rules creation organisation.

That leaves the question, since whether new members should be added to the P5 has been looked at, whether all five members should still be on the United Nations Security Council. Three members are clearly less powerful than when the body was created, with: the USSR now as the Russian Federation; and Britain and France having lost their empires. It is therefore not inappropriate to question whether those three members, accepting that the United States of America and China are still very clearly superpowers, should continue to be permanently represented. It appears, by a not too narrow margin, that the answer should be that all three remain. The Russian

Federation is still deploying its military globally, engaging actively in Europe and the Middle East. France still has deployments in Africa and the reach of the United Kingdom has been documented already (above). All three still possess nuclear weapons within the boundaries of the Treaty on Non-Proliferation of Nuclear Weapons. Their military reach and nuclear arsenals are also matched by the cultural influence and technical knowhow that provides them all with both soft power and means that they are global security threats in the virtual sphere as well. That military and nuclear threat mean that they, along with China and the United States of America, are clearly beyond all other countries in their ability to engage in warfare and therefore, both their abilities to physically enforce agreements and create warfare globally are more than any other countries. That means that, if the United Nations Security Council is to reflect the reality of power globally, which it has to do to remain relevant as countries will just use force to resist if not, then those five current permanent members still need to keep some form of representation.

The British seat, given that this is a policy paper on CANZUK, could, however, be reformed to better represent the situation in foreign policy. This is working under the previously stated assumption that this would take place after the previous policies in the paper, most notably the over the horizon security guarantees, have been implemented by CANZUK and following increased cooperation on a case-by-case basis on other foreign policy matters, such as Hong Kong and other current events at the time. The intention is CANZUK will be acting cohesively on a large range of foreign policy issues. This could be confirmed at the United Nations. However, in doing so, the previously argued for balance between the benefits of acting as CANZUK and the independence of each kingdom needs to be maintained.

One way this could be done is by copying how the USSR and a small number of its internal republic approached the United Nations. Despite being a part of the Soviet Union, Ukraine and Belarus were represented separately outside the Security Council and were full members of the United Nations in its own right, voting separately in all other places, such as the United Nations General Assembly. This model could be reapplied to CANZUK. Each of the four kingdoms could be an independent member state of the United Nations, sitting and voting separately in the General Assembly, being separate for the purpose of the Human Rights Council and other United Nations bodies. They would only be represented by CANZUK on the Security Council, with the seat being held by the United Kingdom being transferred to CANZUK as a successor, just as the USSR transferred its seat to the Russian Federation. This would provide each kingdom a greater position in the United

Nations. It would fulfil the ambition of the three new kingdoms in their quest to be members of the Security Council and would give the United Kingdom the added legitimacy of being a much larger state, with even more military presence than at present. It would therefore mean that the input of the United Kingdom would be wider as the other permanent members would, through the increased military strength, be forced to add more weight to the views of CANZUK. This would further help CANZUK cooperation by having it formerly recognised as a body of representation and could provide the basis for representation of other groups, with it being a potential way (if those involved so chose or wish to) of France to cede its United Nations Security Council seat to the European Union whilst each European Union member remains independent in other United Nations bodies. However, that is beyond the scope of this policy paper and a choice for the French and peoples of the European Union, not the Anglosphere, to decide.

This change in seat control is based upon the understanding of the shared identity across the CANZUK Kingdoms. The basis of this identity in the Anglosphere (as described above) is also the basis of trust and commonality. It is accepting that shared identity that will allow this to work on two fronts, those being the similarities which means that voting should not be difficult and allows for the trust required to share a vote.

Centre for Liberty Report on CANZUK

It should be expected that tension and division on which way to vote in the United Nations Security Council will be minimal, if not non-existent. By virtue of being a part of a wide creedal identity, there is a large amount of common belief. If those beliefs did not exist, the basis of the identity, both what makes the perception of CANZUK as united and unique (two qualities needed for an identity), would not exist. It is therefore the foundation not as a purely cultural or linguistic identity but a shared set of beliefs that make CANZUK citizens united that means that there is little difference in foreign policy. All four CANZUK Kingdoms have a strong belief in democracy, the rule of law, liberty and tolerance. As a result, each kingdom's government and the voters within have similar attitudes, beliefs and desires for foreign policy. That shared basis of creedal identity means that the four kingdoms have similar ambitions, objectives and desired methods in international engagement and therefore, the likelihood is that, on United Nations Security Council issues, which tend to be focused upon the big issues of global importance, each kingdom will tend to agree with each other. That common basis of belief coming from shared identity means that there should not be too much scope for dispute over which way to vote on resolutions if the four CANZUK Kingdoms shared a seat. The second way the shared identity helps is with trust. Shared identity (as covered above) helps increase trust between individuals (Barr, 2003) (Blouin and Mukand, 2019), which will help with ensuring that the governments both individuals involved and the governments at large can trust each other. This should help with engagement. That trust, along with the main Anglospheric republic (the United States of America), allows already for intelligence agreements, such as Five Eyes. The identity, for the creation of trust and advancing all four CANZUK Kingdoms objectives, is crucial for a shared United Nations Security Council Seat to work functionally.

It also works the other way, with the shared seat being a recognition of the common identity. The citizens of the CANZUK Kingdoms are the same people just separated by oceans (as argued above). What makes a Canadian a Canadian, Australian an Australian, New Zealander and New Zealander and a Brit a Brit are the same things. If all four countries were geographically linked, it would be one compact nation and it would be sensible to call for the creation of a nation-state. It is only geography that does not allow for that. Combining the four CANZUK Kingdoms into one United Nations Security Council seat would be a recognition of that shared identity, observing that they are the same people and therefore, should be represented as one where sensible. The demonstration of unity of people would further reinforce the Anglsopheric identity in the branch that is found in the CANZUK

Centre for Liberty Report on CANZUK

Kingdoms, with all the social and economic benefits thereof within each kingdom that come with people believing that they are one united identity (as stated above). Just as bordering territories that share an identity merged in the 19th century, such as Germany and Italy, the CANZUK Kingdoms can combine at the level that is appropriate for the geographic realities.

Once the mixture of commonality of beliefs and identity is accepted as allowing for cooperation on a shared seat in the United Nations Security Council, there would still need to be some technical details that should be addressed. The appointment of the shared ambassador to the Security Council should be one that is approved by all four kingdoms' governments but very much should be the representative of CANZUK, rather than a pawn of the kingdom over origin. Furthermore, it would be advisable that the permanent representatives to the United Nations for each kingdom should meet as a collective with the shared ambassador on a regular basis, with having offices shared between the representatives of the four kingdoms to help with the smooth operation of the joint seat being preferable. The exacts of the mechanisms to decide which way the CANZUK ambassador to the United Nations Security Council would have to be decided by the governments between themselves but given the similarities (argued above), this should not be needed that often as consensus alone would dictate the vast majority of votes. The final technical point is that CANZUK Kingdom should apply under a name beginning with 'U', most likely 'United Kingdoms of: Canada; Australia; New Zealand; and Great Britain and Northern Ireland' (with whether the colon should be removed and the semicolons replaced with commas, requiring an Oxford comma to make it the 'United Kingdoms of Canada, Australia, New Zealand, and Great Britain and Northern Ireland' a tedium for another place than this report) due to the benefit of how it would place CANZUK in the presidency order. The order of which country is president of the United Nations Security Council is done through alphabetical order, with the presidency changing each month. At the moment, apart from the rare times that the United Republic of Tanzania are on the United Nations Security Council, the United Kingdom is currently always followed by the United States of America as president. The two countries usually cooperate with each other as Anglospheric powers to help give a better chance to get their shared objectives achieved during their presidencies (Greenstock, 2016, p.52). Being on the security council under that shared name would allow for those two branches of the Anglosphere to continue to cooperate through that mechanism.

What all of that would allow for is a recognition of the shared objectives of the CANZUK Kingdoms on the United Nations Security Council. The added legitimacy of having all four CANZUK Kingdoms together on the Security Council will improve the influence of the collective in their dealing with the United Nations and provide a further forum to achieve the shared foreign policy objectives beyond the over the horizon security guarantees. By having a united Security Council seat but being independent member states of the United Nations, making them separate in the other organs, the balance between the benefits of uniting on foreign policy points and the independence of each kingdom will be protected, with each kingdom capable of voting differently to each other in all other United Nations bodies, such as the General Assembly.

However, the government of the United Kingdom may be unwilling to share such power, which is why it is likely that the transfer of the United Kingdom's United Nations Security Council seat to a CANZUK as a whole would come along with other United Nations reforms that the United Kingdom supports.

This part will therefore be a suggestion of what a reformed United Nations Security Council may look like. The emphasis should be placed on how this is very much speculative as one potential look with (as stated above) the need to negotiate with so many different states meaning that the outcome of any United Nations reform is not knowable. This part of the policy paper is to demonstrate what level of ambition should be taken into any reform discussions rather than be prescriptive in either what outcome should be expected or what should exactly be called for by the CANZUK governments.

The main place for reform is the United Nations Security Council. The size of the body and why increasing it would likely lead to it being less efficient has already been dealt with (above). This is why suggestions such as those made by Sierra Leone on behalf of the African group, which 'demands no less than two permanent seats, including the veto power, if it remains, and five non-permanent seats.' (United Nations, 2018) There are three main problems with this. The first, being the purpose of the United Nations Security to actually achieve actions, thereby requiring those states capable of military action in everywhere and mass destruction being permanent members, rather than an inactive and unimportant body that only produces theoretical ideas necessitates that the permanent members need to meet the aforementioned criteria (as argued above). Therefore, the suggestion of having countries other than those already (with the change to CANZUK and potential reform of the French seat to include a wider cohesive body) in the Permanent 5 is undesirable. The second point (again argued above) is that growing the size of the organ will not help it. Thirdly, there should be a move away from the overarching dominance of the Permanent 5, with reform to the veto needed.

Centre for Liberty Report on CANZUK

How the role of the Permanent 5 should change requires some expanding. It is clear that they need a prominent and powerful role within the United Nations Security Council as they are the most capable, at the global level, to deploy force and therefore, to not have them heavily in the process would be to either not have access to the most powerful globally deployable militaries or make ignoring United Nations Security Council Resolutions and act with force without legal authorisation the rational option, undermining the ability to create peace. However, it has become clear that the veto is overbearing in power, with the United Nations very neatly fitting into Fukuyama's category of 'vetocracy' (Fukuyama, 2014, pp.488-505). The power of veto has stopped meaningful action being taken in Syria, Burma and Hong Kong. Therefore, some level of change is needed, even if the basic components are already in place, to make the organ effective.

The abolition of the veto has been suggested by a multitude of countries (United Nations, 2018) but this would not be approved by the current holders of the vetoes. Therefore, some form of compromise needs to be created to make any sort of change. Furthermore, if a majority of those powers were against a solution, they would be capable of physically stopping it. To not provide them with a mechanism to be able to block solutions would be to have an unstable international organisation without the ability to stop the great powers being at odds with its rulings, potentially rendering the United Nations even less authoritative and capable of stopping violence than currently.

A balance could be achieved by replacing the veto power with a requirement for a majority of the P5 to vote for a resolution. The way a resolution would work in that situation is that all member states would declare their vote as normal, with the votes recorded. A resolution would require both a majority of the P5 and the whole 15-member body to pass. The votes of the P5 would count towards that overall total, so that in the case of a slim majority against a resolution amongst the elected members, the resolution may still pass with P5 support as is the case at the moment (when all P5 members agree but a slim majority of elected members oppose). This would, by majority vote, provide the P5 with a collective veto. This would still ensure that resolutions do not pass without a majority of those crucial powers supporting them whilst also removing the ability of one country to block a resolution on their own. It would redress the balance of power somewhat whilst still providing the greatest power the largest legal say over international issues.

This, obviously, would need to get passed a number of stages to be implemented but when seen alongside CANZUK having the over the horizon security guarantees limiting the power of the vetoes to begin with, there is a chance that this, with some negotiation, could be agreeable. Faced with the prospect of not being able to use the United Nations to stop CANZUK intervention in countries who have signed treaties and an ineffective body, there would be pragmatic pressure on other members of the P5 to support reform. Beyond that, if the United Nations Security Council is not reformed, its ability to stop conflict will be diminished, adding pressure to governments in developing countries to join the CANZUK over the horizon security guarantee. Even anti-democratic governments may, if the United Nations continues to prove to be incapable Due to the control of the 'vetocracy' (Fukuyama, 2014, pp.488-505) to intervene to stop violent, illegal insurgencies, even anti-democratic governments may start to build the infrastructure and conditions needed for democracy within the CANZUK over the horizon security guarantees to avoid the threat of violent overthrow and the consequences thereof to the individuals in government. In the long term, they could be left with the choice of either leaving the agreement, with the consequences of that (see above), or have to, in the long term, transition to democracy. With that happening, the conditions could be set to 'neutralize existing political stakeholders holding vetoes over reform' (Fukuyama, 2011, p.456), as the United Nations Security Council veto can stop CANZUK intervention in fewer countries. With the prospect of either a growing CANZUK influence or accepting reform to the veto, which option the rest of the P5 would choose is unknown but both are desirable, compared to the present situation, for CANZUK.

That reform would unblock the United Nations Security Council, ensuring that resolutions can pass, unless there is a majority of great powers in disagreement. However, it is not the only potential reform that could come to the organ. There is also potential for reform within the elected members as well. The point on how it is those who are powerful enough to enact resolutions should be those who make it has been expanded at length (see above). To help fulfil that, whilst keeping the number of members on the United Nations Security Council low (for reasons argued above), there could be different members dependent upon which region the resolution is about. It is fairly obvious that countries within a region are more likely to be able to deploy substantial military force within their own region than others and are therefore more capable of aiding the United Nations resolutions in their own region than in others. Furthermore, common sense dictates that in most cases, governments are more interested in issues pertaining to their own geographic region than others because of the physical proximity increasing the threat. Therefore, having a mechanism to increase participation from member states within the region that a proposed resolution concerns would be desirable and increase the potential effectiveness of said proposed resolution. One way this could be achieved is (if the Eastern European region is combined with the Western Europe and Others group and have their seats merged) to remove one seat from each of the existing regions and elect five bonus member states for each region, with votes only being cast from members in the region, rather than the whole international community. Those bonus regional states would only sit as a part of the United Nations Security Council when the resolution being debated and voted upon is directly about the said region. What that would mean is that the composition of each vote would consist of the five great powers (who have a majority vote to veto the resolution), five member states elected for representing the international community and five representatives of the geographic region. That would reflect the balance of interest between the global military powers, international community at large and regional representatives which would help the necessary balance of power to achieve a resolution by the United Nations Security Council which would both be legitimate and enforceable. It should be hoped that the extra interest that each state has in its own region should mean that this proposal, which would increase the power of each state within their region – through providing them with a larger amount of the vote for members on matter only concerning their own region and giving each region a larger number of representatives on matter in their own region – would give member states influence that they desire whilst keeping the aforementioned benefits of the P5 and leaving some influence for the international community at large.

Such changes to the United Nations Security Council's non-permanent member composition will not happen without wider reforms, such as the permanent five reform. Just like with shifting the United Kingdom's seat to CANZUK, any changes to the elected members would require a wider set of amendments, such as the change to the veto (as described above) and a move to CANZUK replacing the United Kingdom (as argued above).

Bearing that in mind, CANZUK, through its association with the United Nations, could change the organisation into an impactful and meaningful body. It would require to propose the supported changes either as a whole or as a part of a set of changes that encompass sorting the main issues discussed (above) and aim at the same level ambition. No individual part of any of the organs of the United Nations, especially the Security Council as the most important, will change without the other parts changing as a part of a compromise. To think that wouldn't be the case would be to assume that vested powers would be willing to act against their own interests, something that does not tend to happen (Fukuyama, 2011, p.456). Therefore, if CANZUK wants to be a part of a strong international rules-based order, proposing the described (above) reforms to the United Nations could be both achievable, as it offers benefits to all involved and gives an option to the dictatorship that do not support Anglospheric values between the (hopefully as described above) growing over the horizon security guarantee agreements and reform of the United Nations, and beneficial to CANZUK.

This should not be seen as the only part of the international community that could be reformed. It would be tedious to use this policy paper to address all international organisations where creating a joint CANZUK approach as a part of a compromise in a wider set of reforms could be achieved. However, the basic principle of the proposals above could be applied in slightly different contexts. That is especially true when the caveat of how that is only a suggestion subject to negotiation and agreement is accepted.

This part of the policy paper has attempted to show how CANZUK cooperation could benefit people globally outside of the four kingdoms through creating better international governance structures. It has emphasised how that can be achieved, with the separate membership of the United Nations whilst having a combined Security Council seat, whilst keeping the independence of each kingdom in almost all foreign policy areas. The final part of the substantive will take the main body of the report into one final direction, that of ultimate trust and cooperation between the four CANZUK Kingdoms.

Centre for Liberty Report on CANZUK

Joint Nuclear Deterrent

This final part of the substantive of this report will focus on what would be the ultimate symbol of trust between the four CANZUK Kingdoms, sharing a nuclear deterrent. This is most certainly not something for immediately, as it will require the most time to physically build and will also necessitate a strong history of cooperation before the governments would be able to coordinate in such a sensitive and dangerous way.

There are four important considerations that are needed when looking at a CANZUK nuclear deterrent are: whether there is a legal justification for it; whether it is necessary for the CANZUK Kingdoms to have a nuclear deterrent; how such a system would be controlled; and why the United Kingdom would agree to sharing a nuclear deterrent given that it is one (all be it one that is near the end of its operational function). They will be dealt with in order as that is the order in which they will need to be justified in public as the legal justification is needed before whether it is needed should be considered, as the legality should be established before whether it is needed can even be looked at. Following that, whether it is needed should be thought through before how it would operate as, if it is not needed, how it would work doesn't matter. Finally, the United Kingdom's government, parliament and citizens would not agree to sharing a nuclear deterrent without knowing how it would operate. Therefore, all four considerations come in a set order and will be dealt with, to explain the necessary chain of logic, in that order.

The first consideration is the legality of such an undertaking. The main question on this front is whether a move would be compatible with the Treaty on the Non-Proliferation of Nuclear Weapons. This is the main, when it comes to the legality of owning nuclear weapons, international treaty on who can own nuclear weapons. Under the current provision, the United Kingdom can own nuclear weapons but the three new kingdoms can't, owing to them having not tested a nuclear weapon before the creation of the treaty (United Nations, 1967). The question is whether the United Kingdom's access to nuclear weapons is enough to allow CANZUK to legally own such systems collectively. This could be achieved if CANZUK can be claimed to be a successor state to the

Centre for Liberty Report on CANZUK

United Kingdom. Successor states have, by precedent, been allowed to carry forward the legal right to nuclear weapons under the Treaty on Non-Proliferation of Nuclear Weapons. This was done by the Russian Federation. Their justification under the Treaty on Non-Proliferation of Nuclear Weapons to owning the nuclear arsenal that they currently own is a continuation as both a government and weapons system from the USSR's operations. The question is whether CANZUK could be claimed as a successor state to the United Kingdom for the purpose of the Treaty on the Non-Proliferation of Nuclear Weapons. This is the justification of the handing over of the United Kingdom's United Nations Security Council seat to CANZUK, so it should be hoped that the same principle is applied to nuclear weapons. However, the United Nations situation is likely to come with other reforms and therefore would be part of a large package of changes. The nuclear situation would be an internal situation for CANZUK without coming as a part of a larger package of reform. Therefore, the willingness and incentive to let any legal questions be ignored for the pragmatic benefits of them won't be present. The main question that is likely to be raised is whether there can be a successor state to a state that still exists. CANZUK will not, and should not, replace the United Kingdom. It will still exist as a legal entity that is a sovereign state. That was not the case with the USSR when it was succeeded by the Russian Federation. Therefore, whether an entity could be a successor state to sovereign state that still exists would require a very large team of international lawyers and even then, it would ultimately be down to the international community and system to decide whether that is acceptable. Although, because it gives legal access to nuclear weapons for all four CNAZUK Kingdoms, it would be the most preferable solution to the question of legality of CANZUK nuclear weapons.

Other solutions are limited, if the first is deemed not legally defendable, which would give a legal justification for access to nuclear weapons for the three new kingdoms. It would be very difficult, if not impossible, for the United Kingdom to provide the three new kingdoms access to their nuclear weapons under Article One of the Treaty of the Non-Proliferation of Nuclear Weapons, which stops those countries (such as the United Kingdom) who already have nuclear weapons transferring 'nuclear weapons or other nuclear explosive devices' to any other state, including giving 'control over such weapons or explosive devices directly, or indirectly' to non-nuclear states (United Nations, 1967). Furthermore, the three new kingdoms have committed, under Article Two to 'undertakes not to receive the transfer from any transferor whatsoever of nuclear weapons or other nuclear explosive devices or of control over such weapons or explosive devices directly, or indirectly' (United Nation, 1967). Therefore, the three new kingdoms need to claim to be a part of a successor state to the United Kingdom for the purpose of control nuclear weapons to be able to have them in a legal manner in accordance with the Treaty of the Non-Proliferation of Nuclear Weapons, with the case (as argued above) being what appears to be the most solidly defendable.

The second consideration is whether CANZUK needs or would want a nuclear deterrent. This comes into the role that is envisaged for CANZUK. If CANZUK is intended to be a serious global power, worthy of a permanent seat on the United Nations Security Council and be an international defender of the rule of law and democracy, it would not only be desirable to help the credibility of CANZUK as a power and for international safety. All of the current permanent five members of the United Nations Security Council are nuclear powers, with the global capability as a state of launching weapons of mass destruction. Therefore, CANZUK having that level of legitimacy of being required on the United Nations Security Council requires it to have the legal authority to own nuclear weapons (and does own), meaning that it can cause mass destruction in all situations at any time and is not in violation of the rules based international order. In that situation, the ability to create global mass destruction in any situation means that CANZUK's inclusion on the United Nations Security Council is necessary. Furthermore, if CANZUK is to be taken seriously by the countries that are treaty to the over the horizon security guarantees, nuclear weapons would be extremely useful. It would demonstrate the power and ability to defend guaranteed states. By being a nuclear power offering to send troops to maintain the government, the guaranteed governments would have more security from external threats, especially other global powers, as attacking troops from a nuclear state is rare from state actors. It would therefore make the threat of invasion from other powers, especially nuclear powers (which are the states with the most access to military force) lower, further helping the security guarantees through acting as a deterrent. These demonstrate that it would be advantageous, due to the impact on the ability of CANZUK to defend their right to the United Nations Security Council and the countries that they will have made treaties to protect, for CANZUK to have a joint nuclear deterrent.

However, having a CANZUK nuclear deterrent may be a necessity for the continuation of long-term peace. Two major global powers have not gone directly to war with each other since the end of the Second World War. This is partially due to the nuclear weapons, which makes war directly between two superpowers unconscionable. Previously, before nuclear weapons, the direct immediate threat to a super power was limited compared to their ability to create destruction across multiple theatres of war. As a result, when global powers intervened in what were, to begin with, regional disputes, they spread to encompass a wider area, opening more theatres of war and creating mass death through conventional weapons. Both the First and Second World Wars started as such, with the former starting as a localised dispute over border and control in the Balkans but became a war that spread not just throughout Europe but created battles in Africa, Asia and even the seas of South America. The latter started, in Europe, as a battle over where the borders of one country, Germany, should be in relation to that of its neighbours. By the end of the war, over (at a conservative estimate) 50 million people had died from conflict alone, even before the disasters that came as a result are added to the total. Whilst these wars eventually became threats to the integrity of the great powers involved, originally, they weren't with the conflicts starting in central and eastern Europe before spreading as the powers involved realised that they could cause damage to their opponents interests in other theatres. Nuclear weapons, by making the first act of war between two great powers directly threatening to the interior of their countries, has eliminated that style of escalation as the first step towards such large conflicts, two great powers going into conventional war against each other, has been made beyond acceptable.

Although, it is also desirable that states that can't cause a great war, the likes of which were seen twice in the 20th century, don't have access to nuclear weapons to ensure because of the potential of nuclear weapons causing an extinction causing event. There is therefore a balance between ensuring that the big powers with the capability of causing mass war have nuclear weapons to make it beyond consideration for them to have a great war and limiting access to nuclear weapons for both rouge states and states small enough that they don't need them, due to the damage that even one mistake can make. Therefore, whether CANZUK needs a nuclear deterrent is dependent on whether CANZUK is a large enough power to cause a global level war. As has been previously established (above), CANZUK will have the power and, where treaties are created, the legal right to deploy across theatres of the conflict on every continent. As a result, CANZUK would be capable of creating the sort of intercontinental war that devastated humanity during the 18th, 19th and first half of the 20th century. CANZUK has the reach to open the number of theatres seen in the Seven Years War. Ultimately, to leave CANZUK without a nuclear deterrent would be to place it in the powerful dangerous position that great states of Europe were in during the 18th, 19th and early 20th centuries, where the ability to gain power through war would not be matched by a large enough deterrent to stop it from being provoked. CANZUK, therefore, needs nuclear weapons to ensure that it can be a part of the nuclear peace. As a result, when balancing stopping states not big enough to be a threat at creating a global war from having humanity ending weapon and having nuclear weapons for states that need them to disincentivise them from creating destruction through conventional war, CANZUK appears to fall on the side of needing to be a nuclear state.

If both want, as a part of being an internationally recognised power, and need due to the level of conventional destruction they could create over a large number of theatres is accepted as leaving CANZUK desiring nuclear weapons, it needs to be established how such a system could operate. Exactly what type of missile deployment system would be used would be down to teams within each government to decide. The main question that can be tackled is who should have the authority to launch such a system. There would be two ways of doing this, either it could be done through required consensus or unilateral request. A unilateral request system would mean that only one of the four CANZUK governments would need to call a strike for it to happen. Meanwhile, a consensus system would require multiple CANZUK governments (whether two, a majority [three] or all four) to authorise a strike. In reality the only time such a weapons system would be launched is in retaliation. At that point, which kingdoms, let alone governments, would still exist is unknown. Therefore, a sensible protocol in the event that a nuclear strike was acted against a CANZUK Kingdom would be to report to any remaining CANZUK government left functional. If such a government still existed, it would be the responsibility of that government to consult to see whether any of the other three kingdoms still had an existing government. If not, it would be down to the remaining government to decide what to do. If more than one CANZUK government still existed, it would be for them to agree what action should be taken. In the event of all four governments being destroyed, then there should (based somewhat upon the current British system) be letters of last resort written by each of the four prime ministers on board each nuclear submarine. The commanding officers would, in that eventuality, be required to take the course of action that best fits the four views expressed, with in the case of direct disagreement (such as one letter calling for immediate retaliation whilst one calls for no retaliation in any circumstances) either what is closest to a majority view being taken. If none can be established, it should be down to the commander of the nuclear system to decide what course of action should be taken. That system would provide control initially to any CANZUK government left standing and if none remained, would provide each government a say in the actions that are taken from that situation. Whilst other mechanisms could be produced, that would be a way of giving the most control to actively operational CANZUK governments and having a mechanism for if none were left.

However, that would be all academic if the United Kingdom was not willing to agree to such arrangements. A large part of this comes to cost. It is claimed that renewing the current nuclear systems the United Kingdom would cost £31 billion, with an extra £10 billion needed as reserves (Defence Nuclear Organisation and Ministry of Defence, 2018), a figure that some claim is beyond reasonable (BBC News, 2017, A). The United Kingdom has a choice over the cost, with it either needing to be completely billed by the British government. In the wake of the covid-19 pandemic the Chancellor of the Exchequer has told the British House of Commons that 'Our public finances have been badly damaged and will need repair.' (Sunak, 2021). Renewing the nuclear deterrent across CANZUK, rather than just in the United Kingdom, would be a set towards limiting spending, with the cost being spread across the four CANZUK Kingdoms. For sharing control with the three new kingdoms, places occupied and governed by the same identity as the United Kingdom, savings for the United Kingdom could be made. This offer of finances is what is most likely to convince the United Kingdom's government to agree to sharing the nuclear deterrent.

If all four of these conditions are met: a legal basis for CANZUK owning nuclear weapons, a need and desire for them being existent; a clear structure of how the deterrent would operate; and British agreement to sharing with the three new kingdoms its nuclear weapons capability then the basis from which a CANZUK nuclear deterrent could be built. It may not encompass all four CANZUK Kingdoms at first. If there are objections from a couple of the new kingdoms, they should not be forced to join. To force them in would be to go against the principles of sovereignty for both the kingdom in general and parliament more specifically of each kingdom, grating against that shared creedal identity. It would be possible to proceed with only two of three kingdoms. That would still provide the benefit, to those kingdoms which agree, of the increase in credibility on the international stage and the decreased chance of them being involved in a war that could spread into theatres outside of where it originated. For that reason, it would be preferable to attempt to get all four CANZUK Kingdoms into the nuclear deterrent system but the process should not be stopped because of objections from one kingdom. The advantages to those which would be willing to join outweigh the disadvantages of not having all four CANZUK Kingdoms involved. It should also, because of that more desirable outcome of all four kingdoms being a part of the nuclear deterrent, be possible to add missing kingdoms later. That would require financial negotiation to make sure that they cover their share of costs of such a program but should not be ruled out due to the advantages of the end goal of all four CANZUK Kingdoms being a part of the nuclear deterrent.

Conclusions

The question of the nuclear deterrent gets to the heart of what this paper's objective, which is to figure out what CANZUK should be. The debate on CANZUK (as argued above) has focused for too long on the British alone and the relationship between the United Kingdom and the European Union. That debate is no longer relevant in the 2020s. With the United Kingdom outside the European Union, that debate is now closed. Therefore, the previous centring of the debate around areas that can replace the European Union is obsolete and irrelevant even in the United Kingdom. If CANZUK as a concept is to remain relevant in the 2020s, the argument for CANZUK and policies proposed for it need to move on.

That is why the nuclear deterrent is important as a concept because it shows the level of ambition for CANZUK going forward. It most certainly would not be the first thing for CANZUK to aim for (as argued below) but demonstrates what CANZUK could become. Whilst claims that 'The CANZUK Union would immediately enter the global stage as a superpower' (Robertson, 2020) may be an exaggeration, the influence and importance of such a project should not be underestimated. If the sensible and achievable steps that balance the priorities of the four CANZUK Kingdoms (as argued above) are followed, CANZUK could be a global force. Superpower may be pushing the limit of that but CANZUK would have the military capability of engaging in multiple theatres of war, the economic strength to build trading blocs to help alleviate poverty and have an important influence on international affairs.

CANZUK should not aim to replace the United States of America as the global superpower of the democratic world. To do so would not only be unachievable but also hinder the goals of the Anglosphere. It cannot be denied that the United States acts differently in international affairs to CANZUK but it has the same aims, such as the spread of democracy, rule of law and limiting of tyrannical power. Promoting those Anglospheric values are the priorities of both the United States and CANZUK, meaning that competition would be damaging to both. CANZUK would provide a strong alternative voice within the Anglosphere, in a position to provide a true source of cooperation.

Neither should CANZUK intend on competing with the European Union. There are differences between

Ciarán Reed

CANZUK and the European Union but a large number of them are irrelevant. This is a key part of drawing CANZUK discussions into the 2020s. Whilst it may have been relevant in the 2010s to compare how the Anglosphere acted and was governed differently to the European Union (Hannan, 2010) (Hannan, 2013) because it was being presented as a choice between the two. That is now no longer the case. Comparison with the European Union's internal model is now no longer needed. The only place where such considerations need to be made is on foreign policy. The European Union may choose to take a different set of priorities. However, given that they are a democratic power, disputes are likely to be limited to approaches on individual issues, with direct disagreement between CANZUK and the European Union unlikely. There is no reason for direct problems because both parties – with limited exceptions: in Northern Ireland over Lough Foyle (BBC News, 2021); Gibraltar (BBC News, 2017, B), where Spain frankly doesn't have a case given both the principle of self-determination and the upholding of international treaties; and the inhabited Rockall Islands, which are disputed by multiple states, some in and some not in the European Union, which is more about fishing rights than anything else (Irish Times, 2019) – don't have much to dispute with each other. Those limited disputes, whilst important in their own rights, are not large enough to cause major problems between CANZUK and the European Union and therefore, there is again no need for competition between the two, especially if CANZUK is to remain relevant as a concept.

Where CANZUK is needed is to be a power that can help resist the growing influence of undesirable governments. China is clearly a force for evil. It is a genocidal (Buckley and Wong, 2021), expansionist (BBC News, 2020, C) regime. It stands against every value that is a part of the identity of the people of the CANZUK Kingdoms. That spreading evil is accompanied by the growing influence and power of the Russian Federation and Iran. The United States, as the sole democratic superpower, has been left unable to aid democratic spread, with failures in Hong Kong, the Arab Spring and Crimea. Blame cannot be solely put on the United States for not stopping these and it is the duty of the rest of the civilised world to aid these situations. To expect the United States of America to be able to deal with all of these situations is to accept that democracy will die and to neglect the duty that reasonable nations have to liberty. Forming a larger power as CANZUK would allow the four kingdoms to be a stronger part of that defence of human decency. It would give a united and stronger front on those issues through which decency can be maintained.

What is yet to be established in this paper is the timescale for achieving that. The order of policies suggested in this paper were not just in the order that best helps move them from the start point of where the debate currently is to where it should ideally go but also the order in which it seems logical for policy to be implemented. Free trade is the policy that will make the largest impact on the daily lives of CANZUK citizens, due to the jobs and wealth it could create. Therefore, priority should be given to it as the most crucial to the lives of the citizens of the CANZUK Kingdoms. Furthermore, it would not make sense to proceed with any of the other policies if free trade was not established, as to trust each other with nuclear weapons but not safety of goods and services would be rather bizarre. The same would go for having freedom of movement but not tariff free trade. As for when it should be implemented, that should be as soon as possible. Given the United Kingdom's application to join the CPTPP is the quickest way to get most of the way to CANZUK trade. The timescale for accession is not clear but on a quick timescale, full accession during 2022 may be achievable given it is an already created treaty, just requiring agreement to British accession and British implementation to happen. Allowing for potential reservations from existing members and problems in implementation at the British end, tariff free trade between the CANZUK Kingdoms through the CPTPP should be achieved by the end of 2023.

The next policy that should be pushed for is free movement. This has to be directly tied to the belief in CANZUK being a cohesive identity. It is perfectly right that both: people should be able to move within their own group's territory; and that nations should be able to control who is allowed into their countries. This is where the emphasis on identity and the shared commonality is necessary, as to not provide a clear answer would be to create the impression of an unfair immigration system. If it just comes across as giving priority to a slightly random set of countries, there would be a fair accusation of it being an unfair system towards other countries. It is only through emphasising that the CANZUK citizens are one people, separated by water, that allows the system to make sense. Therefore, whilst emphasising the common identity will help the four kingdoms in general, due to the benefits of trust and democratic accountability (as argued above), it must be done in time and believed by large swathes of the populations to make the system work. That will be helped by the increase in trade which should take place following the United Kingdom's accession to CPTPP (which should increase interactions between citizens of the four kingdoms, making similarities more obvious), which means that free movement should come afterwards.

The main deadline for that is the end of Queen Elizabeth II's reign. Prime Minister Jacinda Arden has said that she'd like to see New Zealand become a republic (Ainge Roy, 2018). Currently, it appears unlikely that such moves will be taken in any of the four CANZUK Kingdoms whilst Queen Elizabeth II still reigns. However, a change in monarch could be the catalyst to a rethink in all four kingdoms about the monarchy. The monarchy (as argued above) is directly linked to both rights and democracy in all four kingdoms due to the power of inheritance over violence and abstract thought. If the link between that is to be secured, the link in identity between all four CANZUK Kingdoms must be clear as well. Free movement will help with that, as it would represent that common identity necessary for the monarchy, rights and democracy. Therefore, the time scale for achieving this goal is not completely known but there is a deadline event where it would be extremely preferable for it to happen, as to not would make defending the real liberties of the four CANZUK Kingdoms more difficult. Only once the identity is secure, with confirmation of that through can the foreign policy flow, as the rest of the policies are contingent upon the identity. Whilst there is a latest date that needs to be done by, the sooner it can be achieved the better. Ideally, an agreement will have been made in time for Queen Elizabeth II's 100th birthday in 2026, if not implemented before such a time. That would provide a realistic timeframe for sorting out arrangements, especially when they can be copied from the TTTA. That will, inherently within it, also secure the rights part of CANZUK for citizens.

The foreign policy will be harder to sort out, especially with the over the horizon agreements as they will involve countries outside of CANZUK. This is not something that should be rushed, as to make a mistake would undermine the credibility of such a system. Whilst it would ideally come after the shared identity had been created, helping with having a shared front, negotiations could start before free movement is established. The hope should be, allowing for those timings, to have the system fully implemented, with a reasonably large number of guaranteed countries and be proven to work by 2030. That would give a significant enough length of time to create treaties and establish that CANZUK can put down rebellions using this system or, at a minimum, deter attempted overthrows of governments. Speed will be needed on this front as democratic retreat will not stop until action is taken and the longer it is left, the more work will be needed to be done and more people will suffer under the oppression of dictatorships.

Given how directly linked United Nations reform is to the over the horizon security guarantees, again, it would have to happen in sequential order. If the foreign policy can be implemented by the end of 2030, United Nations reform should be started, given the advantages it gives (as argued above), as soon as possible. Ideally, it should be completed by 2035. That gives ample time for CANZUK to join the United Nations Security Council and sort agreement with other member states to reform the body. If that cannot be completed within 5 years, it is probable that it will never be able to be completed.

That leaves the final policy, nuclear weapons integration. This would happen after the United Nations Security Council had a CANZUK permanent seat, along with whatever other reforms could be negotiated. Before that point, the full commitment to having a homogenous front is not present. All four CANZUK Kingdoms would still have free control over absolutely every decision in their name, as they would be individual signatories to each over the horizon treaty and would have the right to not sign individual guarantees. The United Nations Security Council seat would be the first time that complete tailorablility would not exist, as they would have one powerful vote, rather than four separate choices. That is the point at which full cooperation and trust would be required as the ability to take a dissenting view on launching a nuclear weapon doesn't exist. Given that change, it would be worth giving some time for cooperation to be fully established and normalised in the United Nations Security Council before CANZUK heads towards a shared nuclear deterrent. If CANZUK can acquire a shared P5 between 2030 and 2035, starting the nuclear project once that is normalised, around five to ten years after such cooperation. It therefore would probably be some point between 2035 to 2045 that such work would start, with the length of time between the start of work and final completion unknowable at this point. Ideally, for neatness's sake, the whole series of projects, from the removal of tariffs between all four CANZUK Kingdoms to having a shared nuclear program would at least have all projects started, if not finished by 2050. Setting such a target is ambitious but provides a somewhat foreseeable timeframe in which CANZUK could be created as not just a trading and identity group but as a global power.

That objective of CANZUK should not, however, be seen as the final end point of the Anglosphere or even the monarchist Anglosphere. The Anglosphere has been a geographical mobile identity since before recorded history, with it moving around in the modern-day Germanic regions before inhabiting parts of the British Isles. From there, it has spread across large swathes of North America and Oceania. Just as the territory that the Anglosphere originally inhabited is no longer inhabited by it, the continuation of this most glorious identity should not just be concentrated in its traditional areas. The over the horizon security guarantees internationally do not prescribe what type of democracy should be implemented in each guaranteed country (see above). However, (as argued above) the end goal of the project is to produce a democracy so secure that it can become a guarantor country. Such countries should not be excluded for not being Westminster style democracies with the same monarchy but should be brought into the system as long as they are such secure democracies that they can be trusted by all parties. However, if a country becomes so secure in a Westminster style monarchy that it is the sole part of its identity, it should not be excluded from CANZUK. Whilst expansionism is most certainly against the spirit of what is being attempted by united CANZUK, which is a consolidation of where that particular strand of the Anglosphere is located, when others are matched, they should not be excluded. An identity only exists when it can be identified. That is to state (as argued above) that an identity requires the group to be united by shared characterises and for those characteristics to make them unique from all other groups. If a country that either currently has the monarchy becomes secure in its values as the source of its identity, then it must be accepted that it is as much a part of the CANZUK identity as someone who can trace their family back through to the Saxon migration to the British Isles. There are no obvious candidates for that at the moment but is the sense of uniqueness is to be recognised, any group that falls into that category of believing the creedal identity that is the monarchist branch of the Anglosphere not as an opinion but as a part of the identity, should be welcomed into CANZUK as an equal partner just as much as the four CANZUK Kingdoms. To not do so in that situation would be to remove the uniqueness of CANZUK and, by extension, eliminate the basis in identity and all the benefits and justifications thereof (see above). Adding eligible countries would be to fit within the tradition of the Anglosphere, a constantly moving identity that has migrated and spread across at least the past two thousand years. The aim of CANZUK is to unite the monarchist Anglosphere and that should include the whole monarchist Anglosphere, whereever it appears.

The prospect of a united monarchist Anglosphere is already concerning China, with the Chinese state propaganda agency the Global Times realising two baseless propaganda diatribes on Five Eyes (Global Times, 2021, A) – the intelligence sharing organisation that includes all four CANZUK Kingdoms and the United States of America – including accusing it is being an 'axis of white supremacy', despite Five Eyes countries having had more ethnic minority leaders and members of cabinet than the Chinese government which is currently actively committing a genocide (Buckley and Wong, 2021). Recent skirmishes with Iran by the United Kingdom (Landale, 2020) also demonstrate that Iran is not too happy about any bloc including the United Kingdom having a resurgence and hatred is still brewing between the Russian Federation and Canada (Reuters, 2021), Australia (McCulloch, 2021), New Zealand (Wall, 2021) and the United Kingdom (Raab, 2021) is still present. CANZUK should see disagreements with such uncivilised, murderous blemishes to humanity as marks of honour. To not dispute and oppose those countries is to demonstrate a clear moral fault to which a creedal national identity could have no pride and any nation should be ashamed of. If there is to be a better future, given the failures seen under both parties that can realistically govern the United States of America during the 21st century, CANZUK needs to create conditions to help spread democracy.

CANZUK is ultimately a positive project. It is an idea that foresees a way of creating a better world through the cooperation of four united countries. It's an idea that rejects the supremacy of race in favour of an identity that manages to both reject race and combine people into a unique and united collective. It is a concept that aims for a world where people are more prosperous and free, through the benefits of free trade and spreading the Anglospheric values. These values are who CANZUK are and a future where these can flourish is one that should not just be desired by CANZUK citizens but by at least the whole Anglosphere, from the United States of

Centre for Liberty Report on CANZUK

America to India, if not the entirety of humanity. CANZUK would be a recognition of the responsibility that all four CANZUK Kingdoms to their own citizens and the moral duty that comes with that internationally.

This paper has set out how that can be achieved. If ambition is not added to the concept of CANZUK, the debate will remain within the context of the United Kingdom in the 2010s, with at best CANZUK only offering the United Kingdom a replacement in tariff free trade and free movement to the European Union. If the idea of a shared identity is to be kept relevant across all four CANZUK Kingdoms in the 2020s it must be explained how there is a shared identity, benefits to the global protection of what we value as a part of that identity and the internal benefits on the protection of our valuable democracy and rights. Time should not be wasted, whilst the idea is still novel, on concepts that are already accepted by the governments of all four CANZUK Kingdoms, such as tariff free trade. Furthermore, ideas that are already gaining traction, such as free movement, should be pushed only as far as is needed to achieve them. To do any more would be to waste time whilst there is attention on the idea and hold back the possibilities of such a union. If CANZUK is to truly become a modern idea for all four kingdoms in the 2020s, it is what it can do outside of the current scope of debate that needs to be emphasised by supporters of

CANZUK. That is not just for the sake of a project proposed by 'desperate third-rate politicians eager for some gimmick to put them in the headlines' (McCullough, 2018) but a concept that, if taken to the full extent, could produce an alliance capable of defending all the values that are inherently worthy by virtue of who CANZUK citizens are. It is a question of who the people of Canada, Australia, New Zealand and the United Kingdom and what they wish to achieve as a people that will determine whether CANZUK happens.

Centre for Liberty Report on CANZUK

Bibliography

Ainge Roy, Elanor. 2018. New Zealand likely to become a republic in my lifetime, Jacinda Ardern says. The Guardian. https://www.theguardian.com/world/2018/mar/30/new-zealand-likely-to-become-a-republic-in-my-lifetime-says-jacinda-ardern

Anderson, Benedict. 1983. Imagined Communities. (Revised Edition, 2006). Verso

Ardern, Jacinda. 2018. New Zealand Prime Minister: "We Are Committed To Closer Relations With UK". (CANZUK International version. Original from The Telegraph). https://www.canzukinternational.com/2019/01/new-zealand-pm.html

Atlas, James. 1989. What Is Fukuyama Saying? And to Whom Is He Saying It? The New York Times. https://www.nytimes.com/1989/10/22/magazine/what-is-fukuyama-saying-and-to-whom-is-he-saying-it.html

Australian Government. 2020 (updated) *Country profile – United Kingdom.* Department of Home Affairs.

https://www.homeaffairs.gov.au/research-and-statistics/statistics/country-profiles/profiles/united-kingdom (B)

Australian Government. 2020 (updated). Country profile – New Zealand. Department of Home Affairs. https://www.homeaffairs.gov.au/research-and-statistics/statistics/country-profiles/profiles/new-zealand (A)

Bagehot, Walter. 1867. The English Constitution. (2001 Oxford Classics, 2009 reprint). Oxford University Press

Barr, Abigail. 2003. Trust and Expected Trustworthiness: Experimental Evidence from Zimbabwean Villages. The Economic Journal. 113(489)

BBC News, 2020. South China Sea dispute: China's pursuit of resources 'unlawful', says US. https://www.bbc.co.uk/news/world-us-canada-53397673 (C)

BBC News. 2015. Is Japan abandoning its pacifism? https://www.bbc.co.uk/news/world-asia-34278846

BBC News. 2017. A guide to Trident and the debate about replacement. https://www.bbc.co.uk/news/uk-politics-13442735

BBC News. 2017. Gibraltar Brexit row: What is the dispute about? https://www.bbc.co.uk/news/uk-politics-39478636 (B)

BBC News. 2019. Mary Rose crew 'was from Mediterranean and North Africa'. https://www.bbc.co.uk/news/uk-wales-47572089

BBC News. 2020. Barbados to remove Queen Elizabeth as head of state. https://www.bbc.co.uk/news/world-latin-america-54174794 (A)

BBC News. 2020. France police security bill: Protests turn violent again. https://www.bbc.co.uk/news/world-europe-55201993 (B)

Bell, Duncan and Vucetic, Srdjan. 2019. Brexit, CANZUK, and the legacy of empire. British journal of politics & international relations. 21(2). pp.367-382

Bell, Duncan. 2003. Mythscapes: Memory, Mythology, and National Identity. British Journal of Sociology 54 (1)

Blouin, Arthur and Mukand, Sharun W. 2019. Erasing Ethnicity? Propaganda, Nation Building, and Identity in Rwanda. Journal of Political Economy. 127(3)

Bolongaro, Katie. 2020. Why Canada's Failure to Win U.N. Security Council Seat Is a Huge Loss for Justin Trudeau. Time. https://time.com/5855483/canada-un-security-council-seat/

Buckley, Chris and Wong, Edward. 2021. U.S. Says China's Repression of Uighurs Is 'Genocide'. New York Times. https://www.nytimes.com/2021/01/19/us/politics/trump-china-xinjiang.html

Burke, Edmund. 1790. Reflections on the Revolution in France. (Penguin Classics 2004 Edition) Penguin

CANZUK International. 2017. Pro-CANZUK Politician Elected As Federal Party Leader.

https://www.canzukinternational.com/2017/05/pro-canzuk-politician-elected-as.html

Clarke, David. 2015. Law vs history: The Bill of Rights 1688 or 1689? Australian Law Journal

Collier, Paul. 2009. Wars Guns and Votes. (2010 edition). Vintage.

Collier, Paul. Hoeffler, Anke and Rohner, Dominic. 2009. Beyond greed and grievance: feasibility and civil war. Oxford Economic Papers, 61(1)

Conservative Party of Canada. 2018. 2018 Conservative Convention – Immigration, Defence and Democratic Reform. https://www.cpac.ca/en/programs/cpac-special/episodes/64121390/

Defence Nuclear Organisation and Ministry of Defence. 2018. The UK's nuclear deterrent: what you need to know. HM Government. https://www.gov.uk/government/publications/uk-nuclear-deterrence-factsheet/uk-nuclear-deterrence-what-you-need-to-know#uk-and-nuclear-disarmament (A)

Department for International Trade (DIT) and Truss, Elizabeth. 2021. UK applies to join huge Pacific free trade area CPTPP. HM Government. https://www.gov.uk/government/news/uk-applies-to-join-huge-pacific-free-trade-area-cptpp

Department for International Trade (DIT). 2019. UK-Australia Mutual Recognition Agreement. HM Government. https://www.gov.uk/guidance/uk-australia-mutual-recognition-agreement (A)

Department for International Trade (DIT). 2019. UK-New Zealand Mutual Recognition Agreement. HM Government. https://www.gov.uk/guidance/uk-new-zealand-mutual-recognition-agreement (B)

Department for International Trade (DIT). 2020. UK-Canada Trade Continuity Agreement. HM Government. https://www.gov.uk/government/collections/uk-canada-trade-continuity-agreement

Department of Home Affairs. 2021. Immigration and citizenship. Australian Government. https://immi.homeaffairs.gov.au/

Deutsche Welle. 2020. CANZUK — Could it be Britain's new EU?. https://www.dw.com/en/canzuk-could-it-be-britains-new-eu/a-55810928

Disraeli, B. 1835. Vindication of the English Constitution in a Letter. (Reprint, 2018, Forgotten Books). Saunders and Otley

Eaton, Mark Ølholm. 'We are all children of the commonwealth': political myth, metaphor and the transnational commonwealth 'family of nations' in Brexit discourse. British Politics 15

Encyclopaedia Britannica, 2021. Sir Edward Coke. https://www.britannica.com/biography/Edward-Coke

Fabricant, Michael. 2017. Comprehensive Economic and Trade Agreement Debate. House of Commons. (9.2.2017). https://hansard.parliament.uk/commons/2017-02-09/debates/B631FA60-75DD-4E84-A136-A12F831420DB/ComprehensiveEconomicAndTradeAgreement

Ferguson. Niall. 2003. Empire. Penguin

Fichte, Johann Gottlieb. 1808 Addresses to the German Nation. (1922 Jones and George translation) Anodos Books

Fichte, Johann Gottlieb. 1808. Addresses to the German Nation. (1922 Jones and George translation) Anodos Books

Foreign ministers of Australia, Canada, New Zealand, and the United Kingdom, and the United States Secretary of State. 2020. Hong Kong joint statement: November 2020. Foreign, Commonwealth & Development Office and The Rt Hon Dominic Raab MP. https://www.gov.uk/government/news/joint-statement-on-hong-kong-november-2020

Forsythe, James. 2013. Colonial rule: Why Aussies, Kiwis and Canadians are running Britain. The Spectator. https://www.spectator.co.uk/article/colonial-rule-why-aussies-kiwis-and-canadians-are-running-britain

Forsythe, James. 2021. The Northern Ireland protocol problem. The Spectator. 13th January 2021

Fukuyama, Francis. 1989. The End of History? *The National Interest*. 16 (Summer 1989)

Fukuyama, Francis. 1992. The end of History and the Last Man. (Twentieth Anniversary Edition). Penguin Books

Fukuyama, Francis. 2011. (British paperback edition, 2012). Profile Books

Fukuyama, Francis. 2011. The Origins of Political Order. (2012 UK Paperback Edition) Profile Books

Fukuyama, Francis. 2014. (USA paperback edition, 2015). Farrar, Straus and Giroux

Fukuyama, Francis. 2018. Identity. Profile Books

Fukuyama, Francis. 2018. Identity. Profile Books

Gay, Oonagh and Maer, Lucinda. 2009. Research Briefing: The Bill of Rights 1689. House of Commons Library. https://commonslibrary.parliament.uk/research-briefings/sn00293/

Geoghegan, Peter. 2020. Adventures in 'Canzuk': why Brexiters are pinning their hopes on imperial nostalgia. The Guardian. https://www.theguardian.com/commentisfree/2020/sep/09/canzuk-brexiters-imperial-canada-australia-new-zealand-uk-empire

Geoghegan, Peter. 2020. Adventures in 'Canzuk': why Brexiters are pinning their hopes on imperial nostalgia. https://www.theguardian.com/commentisfree/2020/sep/09/canzuk-brexiters-imperial-canada-australia-new-zealand-uk-empire

Global Times. 2021. Five Eyes today's axis of white supremacy. https://www.globaltimes.cn/page/202102/1216338.shtml (B)

Global Times. 2021. Five Eyes' narrow hegemony caters to biased interests of small circle. https://www.globaltimes.cn/page/202102/1216809.shtml (A)

Government of Canada. 2021. Immigrate to Canada. https://www.canada.ca/en/immigration-refugees-citizenship/services/immigrate-canada.html

Greenstock, Jeremy. 2016. Iraq: The Cost of War. (Paperback, 2017). Arrow Books

Hannan, Daniel. 2010. The New Road to Serfdom: A Letter of Warning to America. HarperCollins

Hannan, Daniel. 2013. How We Invented Freedom and Why It Matters. Head of Zeus

Hannan, Daniel. 2016. Are we a nation? https://www.youtube.com/watch?v=wt0__X-Be8k (A)

Hannan, Daniel. 2016. What Next. Head of Zeus. (B)

Hannan, Daniel. 2018. Address to the Conservative Party of Canada Conference. https://www.youtube.com/watch?v=Y4TKkpOQ6Oo

Hannan, Daniel. 2018. Britain is an island of contentment in an EU driven by Brussels to populist revolt. Telegraph. https://www.telegraph.co.uk/news/2018/09/09/britain-island-contentment-eu-driven-brussels-populist-revolt/ (A)

Harding, Luke. 2012. Jamaica to become a republic, prime minister pledges. Guardian. https://www.theguardian.com/world/2012/jan/06/jamaica-republic-prime-minister

Hayek, Fredrich. 1944. The Road to Serfdom. (Routledge Classics Edition, 2001) Routledge

Hellemans, Staf. 2020. Pillarization ('Verzuiling'). On Organized 'Self-Contained Worlds' in the Modern World. The American Sociologist. 51

Home Office. 2020. The UK's points-based immigration system: policy statement. HM Government. https://www.gov.uk/government/publications/the-uks-points-based-immigration-system-policy-statement/the-uks-points-based-immigration-system-policy-statement

Irish Times. 2019. Who owns Rockall? A history of disputes over a tiny Atlantic island. https://www.irishtimes.com/news/politics/who-owns-rockall-a-history-of-disputes-over-a-tiny-atlantic-island-1.3919668

Jones, Dan. 2012. The Plantagenets. (William Collins Edition, 2013). HarperPress

Judah, Ben. 2020. The liberal case for CANZUK. Open Canada. https://opencanada.org/the-liberal-case-for-canzuk/

Landale, James. 2020. Iran attack: How much influence does UK have in US-Iran crisis? BBC News. https://www.bbc.co.uk/news/uk-51038802

Law Reform Commission of Western Australia. 2002. 30th Anniversary Reform Implementation Report. https://www.lrc.justice.wa.gov.au/_files/30th_Report.pdf

Locke, Geoffrey. 1989. The 1689 Bill of Rights. Political Studies, XXXVII

Luce, Edward. 2017. The Retreat of Western Liberalism. (Paperback edition, 2018). Abacus

Madden, P. How Anglo is Australia? 18th April 2013. Parramatta: NSW Community Relations Commission.

McCulloch, 2021. Australia joins calls for Navalny release. Canberra Times. https://www.canberratimes.com.au/story/7111414/australia-joins-calls-for-navalny-release/

McCullough, John, James. 2018. Should Canada, Britain and Australia join together? https://www.youtube.com/watch?v=jFl3OaBi8FY

Miguel, Edward. 2004. Tribe or Nation? Nation Building and Public Goods in Kenya versus Tanzania. World Politics. 56(3)

Mortimer, Ian. 2007. The Fears of Henry IV. (2008 edition). Vintage Books

Murray, Douglas. 2017. The Strange Death of Europe. (Paperback edition. 2018). Bloomsbury

Murray, Douglas. 2019. The Madness of the Crowds. (2020 Edition). Bloomsbury Continuum

New Zealand Government. 2015. Bill of Rights 1688. (Reprint as at 26 March 2015).

https://www.legislation.govt.nz/act/imperial/1688/0002/latest/DLM10993.html

New Zealand Immigration. 2021. Good character for residence visas. New Zealand Government. https://www.immigration.govt.nz/new-zealand-visas/apply-for-a-visa/tools-and-information/character-and-identity/good-character-residence (A)

New Zealand Immigration. 2021. Visas & citizenship. New Zealand Now. https://www.newzealandnow.govt.nz/move-to-nz/new-zealand-visa (B)

NTI. 2019. India. https://www.nti.org/learn/countries/india/nuclear/#:~:text=India%20possesses%20both%20nuclear%20weapons,Test%20Ban%20Treaty%20(CTBT).

On Think Tanks. 2020. CANZUK International. https://onthinktanks.org/think-tank/canzuk-international/

Paterson, James. 2016. Senator Paterson on Brexit. Australian Senate. YouTube. https://www.youtube.com/watch?v=Hqapwe0drnk

Paterson, James. 2020. A Ripper Deal The case for free trade and movement between Australia and the United Kingdom. Adam Smith Institute

Reuters. 2021. Canada condemns verdict against Kremlin critic Navalny, calls for release of protesters. https://www.reuters.com/article/us-russia-politics-navalny-canada-idUSKBN2A22R6

Ricardo, David. 1817. On the Principles of Political Economy and Taxation. (First American Edition. 1819). J. Milligan.

Robertson, Andrew. 2020. The Wall Street Journal: "It's Time To Revive The Anglosphere". CANZUK International. https://www.canzukinternational.com/2020/08/wall-street-journal-its-time-to-revive-the-anglosphere.html

Rosidell, Andrew. 2021. CANZUK: The Next Step in our post-Brexit Journey. Conservatives Global. https://conservatives.global/canzuk-the-next-step-in-our-post-brexit-journey/

Roussinos, Aris. 2020. Why 'CANZUK' is an absurd fantasy. UnHerd. https://unherd.com/2020/08/why-canzuk-is-an-absurd-fantasy/

Rowntree, Seebohm. 1910. Land and Labour in Belgium. Quoted in: Hellemans, Staf. 2020. Pillarization ('Verzuiling'). On Organized 'Self-Contained Worlds' in the Modern World. The American Sociologist

Rudd, Kevin. 2019. Think the Commonwealth can save Brexit Britain? That's utter delusion. The Guardian. https://www.theguardian.com/commentisfree/2019/mar/11/commonwealth-save-brexit-britain-utter-delusion-kevin-rudd

Scheer, Andrew. 2016. A strong Britain is an independent Britain. National Post. https://nationalpost.com/opinion/andrew-scheer-a-strong-britain-is-an-independent-britain

Scruton, R. 2017. Politics Needs a First-Person Plural. The Conservative. 5.

Scruton, Roger. 2006. A Political Philosophy: Arguments for Conservativism. (New Edition, 2019). Bloomsbury Continuum

Scruton, Roger. 2014. How to Be a Conservative. (New Edition, 2019). Bloomsbury Continuum

Scruton, Roger. 2017. Politics needs a First-Person Plural. The Conservative. 5

Seton-Watson, Hugh. 1977. Nations and States: An Enquiry into the Origins of Nations and the Politics of Nationalism. (2019 Routledge edition). Routledge.

Seymour, David. 2019. The time is ripe for a new partnership between the UK, Canada, Australia and New Zealand. Brexit Central. https://brexitcentral.com/the-time-is-ripe-for-a-new-partnership-between-the-uk-canada-australia-and-new-zealand/

Skinner, James. 2018. British MP Proposes Shared UN Security Council Seat With CANZUK Countries. CANZUK International. https://www.canzukinternational.com/2018/05/british-mp-un-canzuk.html (B)

Skinner, James. 2018. Why CANZUK? CANZUK International. https://www.canzukinternational.com/why-canzuk (A)

Skinner, James. 2020. Establish free movement & trade agreements with Canada, Australia & New Zealand. UK Government and Parliament. https://petition.parliament.uk/petitions/554372

Smith, Anthony. 1991. National Identities. University of Nevada Press

Smith, Mathew. 2020. New Zealand is Britons' favourite country. YouGov. https://yougov.co.uk/topics/travel/articles-reports/2020/10/26/new-zealand-britons-favourite-country?utm_source=twitter&utm_medium=website_article&utm_campaign=Britons_favourite_countries

Spiecker, Ben and Steutel, Jan. 2001. Multiculturalism, pillarization and liberal civic education in the Netherlands. International. Journal of Educational Research.

Starkey, David. 2015. Magna Carta. Hodder & Stoughton

Stephenson, Neal. 1995. The Dimond Age. Bantam Spectra

Sunak, Rishi. 2021. Economic Update speech. House of Commons: Westminster (11th January). https://www.gov.uk/government/speeches/economic-update-speech

United Kingdom Parliament. 2020. CANZUK leaders to request Special Envoy for Hong Kong. Parliament Committees. https://committees.parliament.uk/committee/78/foreign-affairs-committee/news/114796/canzuk-leaders-to-request-special-envoy-for-hong-kong/

United Nations. 1967. Treaty on the Non-Proliferation of Nuclear Weapons. https://www.un.org/disarmament/wmd/nuclear/npt/text

United Nations. 2015. History of the UN. https://www.un.org/un70/en/content/history/index.html

United Nations. 2018. Member States Call for Removing Veto Power, Expanding Security Council to Include New Permanent Seats, as General Assembly Debates Reform Plans for 15-Member Organ. https://www.un.org/press/en/2018/ga12091.doc.htm

Vanderstraeten, Raf. 2002. Cultural values and social differentiation: the Catholic pillar and its education system in Belgium and the Netherlands. Compare. 32(2)

Vucetic, Srdjan. 2011. The Anglosphere: a genealogy of a racialized identity in international relations. Stanford University Press

Wall, Jason. 2021. New Zealand calls on Putin to release detained Russian Opposition leader Alexei Navalny. NZ Herald. https://www.nzherald.co.nz/nz/new-zealand-calls-on-putin-to-release-detained-russian-opposition-leader-alexei-navalny/ZYPLRVFBAQOZ736TT74BGECQJQ/

Wintle, Michael. 2000. Pillarisation, consociation and vertical pluralism in the Netherlands revisited: A European view. West European Politics. 23(3).

Printed in Great Britain
by Amazon